# PRAI
# INTELLIGE

*"I've long believed that investors shouldn't rely on uncertain capital gains to live on during retirement. Steve Booren's* Intelligent Investing *reminds us that a great way to work toward a prosperous retirement is with a portfolio of dividend stocks that seek to stay ahead of inflation with a goal of providing steadily growing income over time."*

**MATTHEW PAULSON**
*Founder, MarketBeat*
*Author,* Automatic Income

*"*Intelligent Investing *is a straightforward guide to getting ready for and thriving in retirement. Like the title suggests, the strategy detailed in the book is a smart way to prepare for your financial future. In fact, I'd say it's the most intelligent way."*

**MARC LICHTENFELD**
*Author,* You Don't Have to Drive an Uber in Retirement *and* Get Rich with Dividends

*"What's the difference between being rich and being wealthy? If richness is fleeting, wealth is lasting. The methods Steve discusses in* Intelligent Investing *can help to create and preserve lasting wealth."*

**LEE BROWER**
*Founder, Empowered Wealth*
*Author,* The Brower Quadrant

*"There are hundreds of books about retirement planning. Steve Booren's book,* Intelligent Investing, *covers the complex topic of retirement income in an understandable, easy-to-read way. Real client scenarios combined with his investment strategy, developed over decades, will inspire thought and conversation about the most important steps in determining your financial future."*

JIM PUTNAM
*Chairman of the Board, LPL Financial*


*"Young investors should focus on growth in dividends and position themselves to invest in dividend stocks that have a high likelihood of increasing dividends in the future. In his book, Steve Booren explains why growing income through intelligent investing is key to retirement success."*

MILLIONAIRE MOB
*Author,* Dividend Investing Your Way to Financial Freedom: A Guide to Live Off Dividends Forever


*"I've had the pleasure of knowing Steve for many years and witnessing his long, successful career as a financial advisor. He uses his knowledge and experience to provide clear, relevant advice on how investors can position themselves to keep income growing, both before and during retirement."*

ANDY KALBAUGH
*Managing Director, LPL Financial*

# INTELLIGENT
## INVESTING

# INTELLIGENT INVESTING

YOUR GUIDE TO A GROWING
RETIREMENT INCOME

**STEVE BOOREN**

Library of Congress Control Number: 2019933224

ISBN Paperback: 978-1-949639-62-9

Cover and Layout Design: Mary Hamilton

*To Marie my biggest fan, my family who brings me delight,*
*and to my clients who I love to serve.*

# YOUR BOOK, YOUR WAY

| | |
|---|---|
| **TEXT** | Thank you for purchasing this book. Additional copies are available at multiple online retailers, including Amazon and our website, www.intelligentinvestingbook.com. |
| **AUDIO** | An audiobook accompanies this text and can be downloaded at www.intelligentinvesting-book.com. |
| **VIDEO** | Video interviews that further cover the concepts in this book are available at www.intelligentinvestingbook.com. |
| **EBOOK** | Download this text's eBook at www.intelligentinvestingbook.com for digital reading and easy sharing. |

# TABLE OF CONTENTS

## Who Am I

## The Why

## Inflation: The Investment Loss You Never See ... Until It's Too Late

## Focus on Income, Not Market Value

## The How, or What Do I Do About It? Show Me!

# FOREWORD

## THE BEST KIND OF PERSON

I've had the great pleasure of working in a strategic position with Steve Booren for over two decades. Through his participation in my entrepreneurial coaching program, I've spent 80 full days with him over the past 20 years, and I can confidently say that Steve is an excellent entrepreneur and a wonderful person, and I'm excited to have been invited to participate in his new book.

This book is chock-full of his knowledge and offers readers an approach to retirement filled with excitement and confidence.

## THREE CRUCIAL POINTS

I want to point out three of the crucial points made in this book. The first is that the earlier you get started with a strategic long-range plan for preparing for retirement, the better off you are.

And it can start today.

The second point is that you not only need to have a sum of money that grows until you reach retirement, you have to have retirement income that grows after you retire.

One of the biggest mistakes people make when it comes to retirement is thinking, "If I have this certain lump sum of money, I'll be okay." This doesn't take into account that the sum gets eaten away every year due to inflation.

Whatever lump sum you have will become less every year between now and the time you retire, and since inflation will continue after you retire, the erosion will continue.

The third point is that very few people can understand the intricacies of investment well enough on their own to achieve those two goals—constantly growing your money until your retirement, and then continuing to grow your money after retirement—and therefore, a knowledgeable, experienced, and totally committed financial advisor is essential in order to do it right.

## PLAYING IT SAFE

Once you retire, you never want to eat into the base you have. You want an amount of retirement funds that generates a cash flow that matches your post-retirement lifestyle goals.

So, you won't be living off of your actual savings but rather the growth of your savings.

Instead of getting in and out of the stock market, you'll be looking at long-term investments that continually grow.

These aren't one-off innovations that will get you rich quick on an investment; they're investments that have been, and likely will be, good for decades.

## STRATEGIC, NOT EMOTIONAL

Planning and investing in this way can mitigate the emotional volatility that comes with other kinds of investing—excitement when your stocks are up, sadness when they're low—which is a trap that a lot of people with retirement income fall into.

You have control over that while you're in your prime income-earning days, while you're still active in your profession. But once you're in your retirement days, the control that you need has to come from the intelligence and the strategic growth of your actual retirement.

## A NEEDED GUIDE

All of these issues point to the fact that you need a guide, both in the sense that you have a person who's going to be with you for the entire game, and also that this individual has a guide that gives you confidence and makes you largely immune to whatever's happening short-term in the economy and the marketplace.

Unpredictable shifts take place in the economy, and regardless of all of the ups and downs, you should always be making progress toward your goals.

I think that the guidance this book provides will be so valuable to you that you won't just read it once, but continually.

The purpose of a guidebook isn't just to help you put a plan together right now; it's to continually make you more capable and knowledgeable so you can recognize that, while there are dangers in the world, you have a strategy to deal with every one of them.

## NO FEAR

The two fears most people have about retirement is that they won't have enough financial resources when they retire, and that they're going to run out of financial resources after they retire.

These are the two greatest dangers and among the reasons why a great financial advisor must know his or her clients intimately in terms of how they see the future and what will make their retirement years more meaningful and enjoyable to them than the previous years.

It all has to start with a financial advisor finding out what your fears are and what opportunities you currently have that you want to take advantage of in your life.

The opportunities aren't about finances, but about the actual life you want to live and about everything that's meaningful to you. These all go down in the plans, which are designed so that you can rest assured and be confident of your future, regardless of what happens in the world outside of you.

You don't want a financial advisor who engages in fear-mongering. When someone actively advertises in a way that creates doubt, fear, and uncertainty, it means they probably have a hidden agenda.

By reading this book, you'll gain a great deal of clarity about the messages you're receiving, and you'll be prepared to engage in planning your retirement from a standpoint of confidence and empowerment, not fear.

A great financial advisor isn't committed to any particular investment. They have criteria that constitute a good investment, which is one that matches up with what you want for your future.

Equipped with the mindsets and insights in this book, you'll be prepared to partner with a financial advisor who will help you create the future you want, not just the future you need.

**Dan Sullivan, Founder of The Strategic Coach Inc.**

# IN GRATITUDE...

First and foremost, I am grateful to the clients I serve. I'm grateful to work with them, walk the path of life with them, listen, laugh, console, cry, celebrate, and to serve them. It is a gift to serve this group of individuals and families like a family.

I am grateful to my team at Prosperion. You make me look good. I tell people I "surround myself with angels", and that is what you are - angels. You extend your service and love to our clients that demonstrates our commitment to Care Beyond Advice.

I am grateful to the advisors at Prosperion. Each of you are unique and offer perspectives based on your years of experience serving clients. I am grateful to you and how you encourage me, inspire me, and grant me grace when my leadership skills are challenged.

I especially want to thank the folks who have helped me in this writing journey. Kyle Haas - you are a rock star. I appreciate your wisdom, patience, coordination, and calm reactions to my random thoughts. To Barbara who did much of the editing, thank you for all your skill and guidance. To Michael for your team helping us to get this book from in my head to in the hands of others.

To my family, I am so grateful for your love for me.

To Marie, the love of my life. You are my biggest fan, my daily sounding board, who encourages me to keep the main thing the main thing.

And to my Lord and Savior, who grants me the breath of life, every day, that allows me to serve and love others.

In gratitude,
Steve Booren

# Who Am I

A little information goes a long way.

Planning for retirement is different for every individual, but I've found that having access to the best financial information evens the playing field. No matter who you are or what your retirement goals are, the more you know, the better the decisions you'll make.

This book isn't about increasing your lifestyle; it's about *maintaining* your lifestyle by *increasing your income*. If you don't grow your income, inflation will chip away at it over time. Think about it: $10,000 in 1980 bought much more than that same $10,000 will buy in 2018. If you don't grow your income, you'll slowly get poorer, and by the time you realize what's happening, it will be too late to do anything about it.

My goal is to give you the information that will empower you to lead the most meaningful life possible and to have your financial resources enable you to have the kind of life you want. Planning for retirement is personal, and together, we will build and maintain a portfolio that suits *your* needs.

## WHAT TO EXPECT FROM THIS BOOK

My goal is to make the retirement process as meaningful and helpful for you as possible, every step of the way. As you shift into retirement, it's time to recalibrate and to figure out how you want to spend these years.

I want to help you realize how critical it is for a portion of your portfolio to contain *growing* income, and the earlier you realize that, the better you can plan for the future—time and inflation wait for no one.

## WHO SHOULD READ THIS BOOK

This book is for anyone who has been accumulating capital and financial assets over the course of a thirty-year career. When you near retirement age, you're in a position to say, "No more working for a paycheck. I want to invest my time in my *avocation*, not my *vocation*." Or perhaps you just want to spend more time with your family. In either case, this is the moment when many people decide to turn *off* their paycheck and trust that their portfolio will sustain them for the next thirty-five or forty years. Think that's too ambitious? Well, as of the publication of this book, one out of every four sixty-five-year-olds will live past age ninety, and one out of ten will make it past ninety-five.

That's thirty potential years *without working*. Do you seriously want to have the buying power of your money decrease in your later years? Do you want your money to run out before you do? Therefore, if your portfolio income is not growing, you're getting poor slowly. We'll get into the details of that shortly, but keep that in mind for now.

The purpose of this book is to help you get clear on *why* and *how* to retire shrewdly. The "why" may sound simple, but it is not. Our media and financial services industry messaging does *not* help investors with the "why," and this is detrimental to investor behavior.

The "how" is our investment strategy here at Prosperion Financial Advisors. Investing in companies that grow their dividends is not a new methodology—look at Warren Buffett, perhaps one of the savviest investors of all time. Buffett runs Berkshire Hathaway, one of the world's greatest investment conglomerates. Consider Buffett's fundamental principles of smart investing:

- Invest in simple businesses that can be explained in a sentence or two and that have a *consumer orientation* (people buy their goods and services).

- Invest in companies that manage their resources intelligently.

- Look for companies that manage their corporate checkbooks like owners—because they *are* owners.

- Invest in companies that make a nice profit and reinvest a portion of that profit back into the company for future growth, while also rewarding the stockholders by paying out a portion of the profits. These companies tend to increase dividends over time.

The key difference between how Buffett manages Berkshire Hathaway and how *we* operate is that he reinvests the dividends back into Berkshire, paying out nothing to shareholders. He believes he can do a better job with the cash that would be sent to shareholders than they could do on their own. That may be true, but few people are in a position to receive no income from their portfolio, especially if they are at a stage of life at which they need to be growing their income.

Like Mr. Buffett, we take a long-term perspective. The daily, weekly, or even annual fluctuations in the market are, for the most part, noise. It takes courage, discipline, and determination to see beyond that noise and remain focused on the end goal—investing in great companies with growing income. My team and I have a methodology for doing this—and it is very effective.

Are you ready?

## ABOUT ME

I am the founder and owner of the investment management and advisory firm Prosperion Financial Advisors in Greenwood Village, Colorado. My team and I have spent the past forty years providing investment management and financial planning advice to individuals, families, and institutional investors. Many investment fads and economic cycles have come and gone during that time, and those fads have negatively influenced investors and client behavior. Nevertheless, we've always been there to help guide our clients through the rough waters and into smoother sailing.

"Personal finance" is a lot more *personal* than it is finance. Every one of our clients is different, with different goals and needs. It's our job to meet them exactly where they are, which we do by asking the right questions, listening to clients' responses, and using that information to create the best plan for *them*.

Smart investing leads to better financial outcomes over the long term, and this book will share my philosophy on smart retirement and improving investment behavior. Ultimately, we want your resources to last longer than you may think is possible. Over a long investment time frame, this will lead to greater prosperity and a wider range of choices for you and your family. To paraphrase Re/Max cofounder and fellow Colorado entrepreneur Dave Liniger, "Everybody wins."

# CHAPTER ONE

# The Why

We believe the only reason people invest is for *income*—either income for today or income for tomorrow. Income for *today* is important to retirees and to anyone else who needs to access cash flow from their investments *now*. Income for *tomorrow* is important to people saving for a time in the future when they will take income from their portfolio.

It is that simple.

We believe people should not spend their *balance* (what their investments are worth); rather, they should spend the *income* generated by their investments. Yet most of the big players in the financial services industry and financial press look at retirement finance from a different perspective—and I believe a misleading one. They view investing as either a net gain or a loss. Whenever we turn on the television, we are reminded of what the market "did" for the day, week, month, quarter, year, and so on. This myopic focus on fluctuation is more about entertainment and generating ad sales for those television shows than about providing solid financial advice.

Tracing market behavior triggers responses similar to drug addiction: When the market's up, investors feel high and unstoppable—and when the market goes down, investors feel withdrawn and upset. It's not a healthy way to approach investing, so we help people with their investment behavior, first by telling them: "Turn off your television! Stop watching the ups and downs!"

What an investment or a portfolio may be worth or how the market did for the day is irrelevant—people do not spend what their investments are worth or what their account is valued at; they spend the income *generated by* their investments.

Why do so few pay attention to growing income? Well, compared to the excitement of the financial markets, growing dividend investments can seem downright dull. And let's face it: boring does not sell. Flashy entertainment sells, and that's what we see everywhere in our investing and financial culture today. (We'll talk more about distractions in chapter five.)

## WHY IS A GROWING INCOME NECESSARY?

It is essential for your income to grow if you want to maintain your purchasing power and keep up with inflation—the rate at which prices for goods and services rise while the purchasing power of a currency falls. Growing your income is important if you want your money to be able to buy as much in the future as it does right now. If your income is not growing, you are destined to have lower purchasing power in the future, meaning you will slowly get poor. Inflation is so sneaky that it is sometimes called the silent financial killer.

Most people aspire to some form of retirement. Retirees do what they *want* to do, on their own terms. For most, this means no longer having to work for a living because they receive income from some other source.

Today, a non-smoking married couple at age sixty has a 90 percent probability that at least one will reach the age of ninety, and the surviving spouse may live five, ten or more years longer. And that's with today's medicine—assuming that medical science doesn't advance in that time! This means you may actually have to rely on some non-working source of income for thirty to forty years or more.

Think back to your first job thirty or forty years ago. Think of the salary you earned. Now imagine living on that same amount of income today. I remember when I was offered a salary of $14,400 forty years ago. It was more money than I knew what to do with. But fast-forward to now: If I were still trying to live on $14,400 a year, I wouldn't be around very long! That's exactly what happens if you don't grow your income during retirement.

## SECURITY VERSUS SAFETY

People confuse *security* with *safety*. We define security as getting the same dollar amount back at the end of a certain period—like putting cash in a vault. Safety, on the other hand, is getting the same *purchasing power* back at the end of a period. Consider the thirty-year salary example above; security is getting that same $14,400 income for thirty years. Bonds are a good example of the importance of this distinction: Why do people think bonds or fixed-income investments are "safe?" For the reasons outlined above, my team and I believe they are "secure" but certainly not "safe." (We'll discuss bonds in greater detail in a moment.)

As I said earlier, following the ups and downs of the market from day to day is confusing and disorienting—some days are up, others are down. When you step back and look at the trends, however, it is obvious that interest rates have fallen dramatically over the past thirty years. Today, interest rates are less than what the inflation rate *appears to be.*

Read that last sentence again and think about what it means. It means many people are putting money into investments from which they will earn *less* than the inflation rate. Getting poor slow is the end result of this.

What is amazing is the financial services industry promotes an investment methodology or belief that as investors age, they should actually shift a percentage of their assets (usually the percentage correlates to their age) from investments that protect you from inflation to investments that do not. In other words, as you age, you would put more of your retirement money into investments that lose purchasing power, namely fixed income or bonds.

A stunning consideration: In 2018, a ten-year US Treasury bond paid around 2 percent. An alternative might be to invest in a basket of companies with global reach, such as an exchange-traded fund that mirrors the S&P 500 Index for example. Some of these pay dividends, and some do not. Either way, the dividend rate on this index is around 2 percent.

Think about that for a moment. You can invest in a basket of companies and earn about the same current income as you would by investing in a "secure" US Treasury bond. When the bond matures in ten years, you get back exactly what you invested—your principal. This is why we describe bonds as "secure"—because you get back your principal. Meanwhile, dividends for the S&P 500 have increased on average 6 percent per year since its inception in 1957 according to data from Yahoo Finance.

Let's look at an example: Assume you've invested $100,000 over a thirty-year time frame. Figure 1.1 is what your income would look like in a fixed-income strategy compared to a growing income strategy:

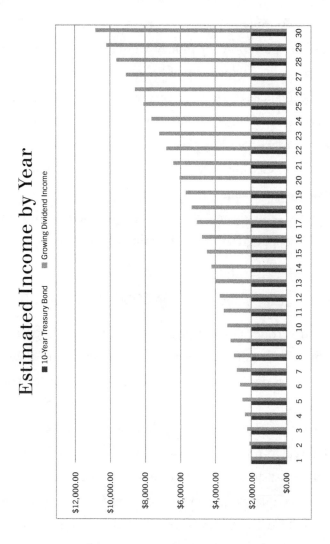

Figure 1.1 Assuming a $2,000 initial investment in a fixed 10-Year Treasury Bond compared to the same investment in a dividend-paying company with a 6 percent dividend growth rate, the long-term historical average for companies in our strategy. This is a hypothetical example and is not representative of any specific investment. Your results may vary.

The math simply doesn't lie.

## DIVIDEND STRATEGY

Bonds are fixed income. "Fixed" means the amount does not increase. If we have any inflation, when the bond matures you will have *less* in purchasing power—your money won't buy the same amount of goods or services it did when you bought that bond.

Yet the financial services industry seems to have a preset mentality that everyone, especially older investors, need fixed income. But fixed income will only doom this portion of their portfolio to a lower purchasing power. Getting back less in purchasing power while relying on retirement assets to generate income is a guaranteed way to lower your standard of living and ultimately get poor slowly. Growing your income is essential given the inevitability of inflation.

## THE PROBLEM WITH FIXED INCOME AND BONDS

Bonds and certificates of deposits (CDs) are promoted by mainstream financial media outlets as safe investments, but they do not grow or increase your income—they quietly rob you of your purchasing power.

Let's look at Tom, one of our longtime clients (all names have been changed to protect the privacy of our clients). Tom spent his entire career as a successful businessman. He understood the value of diversification, quality, and owning a portfolio of companies, not just a portfolio of stocks. However, Tom believed he needed more bonds as he grew older, a rule of thumb that may sound good but actually sets people up for disastrous results. We advised against acquiring more bonds, but he moved forward against our plan anyway. Here's what happened:

In 1995, Tom sold his company at age sixty-five. Now he was ready to enjoy his retirement—visiting grandchildren, traveling the world, and simply taking it easy. Tom and his wife were healthy and loved adventurous travel. Upon his retirement, he insisted (against our advice) that we invest 60 percent of his $3 million portfolio in bonds, and 40 percent in growing dividend companies. This is a common belief that as you age, you should allocate a percentage of your portfolio to bonds that is equal to your age (e.g., if you're sixty years old, 60 percent of your investments should be in bonds). Therefore, the older you get, the higher the percentage you should have in bonds—or so the adage goes. Supposedly, this is a conservative move to keep your money from disappearing. But that's a *terrible* rule of thumb because bonds *never increase in income*. Need more proof? Here's the rest of Tom's story:

As time passed, we urged him *not* to increase his allocation to fixed income and to keep at least 40 percent invested in companies that paid and grew their dividends. Figure 1.2 shows what his income looked like by decade:

| YEAR | BOND YIELD | BOND EARNINGS | DIVIDEND YIELD | DIVIDEND EARNINGS | TOTAL EARNINGS |
|---|---|---|---|---|---|
| 1995 | 7.8 % | $93,000 | 3.5 % | $28,000 | $121,000 |
| 2005 | 4 % | $48,000 | 3.5 % | $56,000 | $104,000 |
| 2015 | 2.5 % | $24,000 | 3.5 % | $112,000 | $136,000 |

Figure 1.2 This is a real-world example provided by a client and used with permission. Your results may vary.

From the bond side, Tom earned $93,000 in 1995. But jump to 2015, and the same amount of money was paying him *$24,000*—75 percent *less* than back in 1995. Thanks to interest rates declining with "secure investments" in bonds, his income actually decreased in the ensuing twenty years.

Now look at what the dividends did for him—they increased, so at least he has more nominal income than when he started, going from $121,000 per year to $136,000 per year. However, if you factor in what inflation did in those twenty years, he has less total purchasing power. So, dear reader, which is safe and which is secure? Bonds are fixed, and in this case, they went down because interest rates fell. And stocks that pay dividends—especially the type that we invest in—are growing dividends. Tom's dividend income has *quadrupled* in a twenty-year period, and he would have done better if he had followed our advice back in 1995.

Today, Tom is eighty-seven and still in good health, but he is unable to travel as much as he and his wife had originally wanted to. We were eventually able to get him to agree to maintain his allocation to growing dividend companies, and that segment of his portfolio now generates $136,000 per year.

His income dropped because he wanted to be "secure" in bonds. Unfortunately, the math doesn't work out. It's all about the income, not about the balance. Figure 1.3 shows what this looks like:

# Inflation

At 3 percent inflation, your $1 buys $0.50 of goods and services in twenty-four years. The average retirement is thirty to forty years.

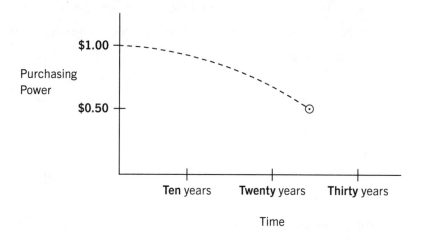

Figure 1.3

## THE RULE OF 72 AND HOW IT DRIVES PURCHASING POWER

You may have heard about the "Rule of 72" when it comes to investing but aren't sure what it means. Using a fixed annual rate of interest, the Rule of 72 simplifies the calculation for how long it will take for an investment to double. By dividing 72 by an annual rate of return—the gain or loss on an investment over a period of time—investors can make a rough determination of how many years it will take for an investment to double in value. For example, one dollar invested at 10 percent would take 7.2 years to become two dollars.

We take the Rule of 72 and apply it to inflation and dividend growth. Growing your income at 5 percent per year, your income doubles in fourteen years; if your income is growing at 7 percent per year, your income doubles in approximately ten years.

15

When you have *inflation*—when there's an increase in the general price of goods and services, say a 3 percent inflation rate—that rule means your money is worth half as much in twenty-four years.

This is critical knowledge for investors, especially when you consider the financial makeup of most Americans. According to the Center on Budget and Policy Priorities:

> Most elderly beneficiaries rely on Social Security for the majority of their income. For 61 percent of elderly beneficiaries, Social Security provides the majority of their cash income. For 33 percent of them, it provides 90 percent or more of their income. Reliance on Social Security increases with age, as older people—especially older women—outlive their spouses and savings. Among those aged 80 or older, Social Security provides the majority of income for 72 percent of beneficiaries and nearly all of the income for 42 percent of beneficiaries.[1]

This may be news for those fortunate enough to receive a pension, but remember: most pension plans *do not* escalate with inflation. This means most American retirees will experience a *declining standard of living* as inflation erodes the purchasing power of their income. Sadly, these folks will realize this is happening to them only after it's too late to make any significant changes. Imagine how it feels to a seventy-five-year-old when he finally recognizes the lousy financial situation he's in—and realizes he's probably got another fifteen years of life ahead of him. Over those fifteen years, his purchasing power will decrease another *37 percent*.

1   Center on Budget and Policy Priorities, "Policy Basics: Top Ten Facts about Social Security," https://www.cbpp.org/research/social-security/policy-basics-top-ten-facts-about-social-security, last updated August 14, 2017.

Inflation is a nasty headwind facing every investor, and a huge wake-up call for retirees or investors who think bonds or other fixed income are "safe." For most retirees their income is derived from:

- Social Security: barely escalates (at the wage base)

- Annuities: the majority do not escalate

- Bonds: fixed income

- Investing in equities (companies) that pay dividends

## Typical Retirement Income Sources

For most retirees, income is acquired from four sources: Social Security, annuities, bonds, and investing in equities. For equities, income is generated by either selling the equity or through the payment of dividends to shareholders.

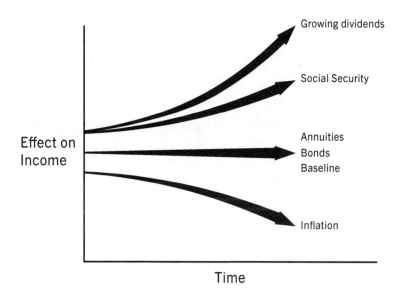

Figure 1.4 This is a hypothetical example and is not representative of any specific investment. Your results may vary.

Figure 1.4 illustrates clearly what I've been saying: If you do not have enough in growing income, you will slowly get poor over time, and you will not realize it for fifteen, twenty, or twenty-five years. And at that point, it is too late.

In the next chapter we'll explore how inflation is the silent killer of most American investors, and what you can do to stop it from getting you.

CHAPTER TWO

# Inflation: The Investment Loss You Never See ... Until It's Too Late

I *nflation*, or the yearly rise in prices of goods and services, is the silent killer of investors everywhere. Here's why: None of us receives a monthly statement that says the purchasing power of our income has decreased due to inflation. However, inflation is noticeable at the grocery store or when the medical bills come due. Everything costs more than it did five years ago. Nor does inflation affect only commodities: property taxes and insurance costs always rise, as well.

If you're heading into retirement, you will feel the impact of inflation acutely, especially when your account statement shows that you've lost a *third* of your purchasing power in the past decade. Now what do you do—are you going to head back to work at age seventy-five? Not likely.

In other words, inflation could *really* make a mess of your retirement if you're not prepared for it, and by the time you see the effects of inflation on your portfolio it's too late to make any substantial changes. In this chapter we'll examine how the government tracks inflation, how the average American deals with inflation, and how you can better prepare for the inevitable consequences of inflation when you plan for retirement.

## THE CONSUMER PRICE INDEX AT A GLANCE

It's hard for the average American to gauge the rate of inflation, but luckily, our government tracks it with the Consumer Price Index (CPI), which measures how prices change from year to year by examining a "basket of products and services" that the average American might purchase, like energy, food, and other commodities. As of the publication of this book, the CPI noted a 2.2 percent rise over the previous twelve months. Figure 2.1 is an illustration of the CPI showing the annual change in prices year by year:

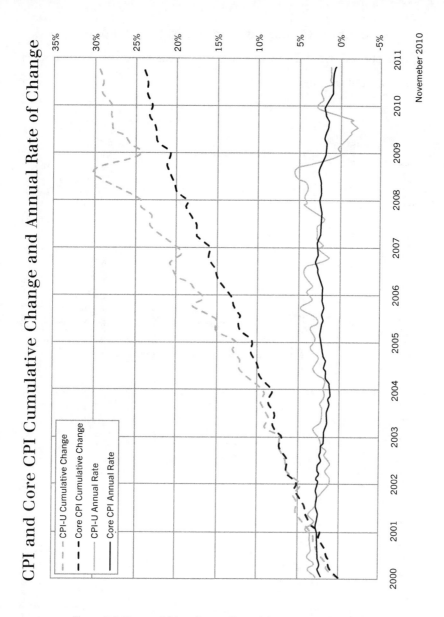

Figure 2.1 Source: Advisor Perspectives, dshort, accessed 2018.

The prices illustrate *compounding* over a ten-year period. The solid lines indicate the slight annual fluctuation of inflation as measured by the CPI. Those dash lines show how inflation is *felt* even if consumers don't see it.

21

Still don't believe that inflation is inevitable? Look at figure 2.2, which shows the decline in the purchasing value of a dollar over *fourteen decades*:

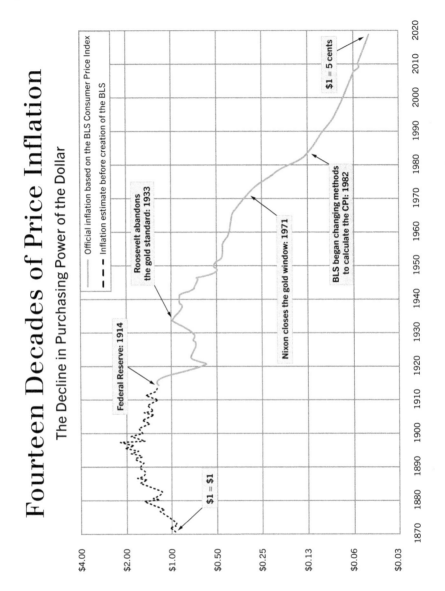

Figure 2.2 Source: Advisor Perspectives, dshort, accessed 2018.

Figure 2.2 shows that over a 140-year period, prices *rose* while purchasing power *decreased*. A dollar from 1870 will only get *five cents'* worth of the same goods and services today.

## THE CPI ISN'T FOOLPROOF

There is some bias in the CPI's interpretation of the data. In the past, the CPI has overstated changes in the cost of living, though much of that has been eliminated in recent calculations. Still, the CPI does not always consider the effect of technological advances in enhancing the value of items in their hypothetical basket of goods and services. For example, cell phones are included in the CPI, but think of the value you derive from your smartphone today as compared to your flip phone circa 2004. The same is true for nearly all consumer electronics.

The CPI is not a 100-percent-accurate measure of inflation, but it is the best measure we have, and it has been used for decades.

## PERSONAL INFLATION RATE

Your personal inflation rate is different from the CPI. If your children are grown—"off your payroll," so to speak—and they've graduated from college, next year's college tuition prices do not affect you. Conversely, your medical needs may be increasing in cost more than others' medical needs.

As you head toward your retirement years, what areas of your life do you expect you will need to pay more for? Leisure travel? Health care? Insurance? Mortgage? Do you think those areas will see any price increases? Your personal inflation rate reflects what you need, consume, and use—and that number may vary greatly from the CPI.

## THE SILENT KILLER, EXPLAINED

How is inflation a *silent killer*? Let's say inflation increases at 3 percent per year. At the end the year, you may notice less money left over at the end of each month. You may also notice your grocery bill increasing even when your purchases have not. Prices just never seem to decline. That is the slow, annual inflation rate at work—the silent killer.

Now let's look at the long-term implications of inflation. When inflation averages 3 percent per year, your purchasing power is cut in *half* in just twenty-four years. Here's another way to understand this: over that twenty-four-year period, prices for goods and services *double, and they triple in thirty-six years.* Retiring at age sixty, your costs have doubled by age eighty-four and tripled by age ninety-six. Is that a far-fetched scenario? Hardly. Three percent is close to the long-term inflation average.

This means if your income is not rising—especially during your retirement—you are going to have a *lower* standard of living in the future and face the possibility of having to go back to work. If you are currently relying on bonds for your income and they are "fixed," the picture is not pretty.

That slow, subtle impact of inflation on the retirement income of average Americans is what we want to change. Every investor needs a strategy to overcome inflation.

## BILL AND BARB: A CAUTIONARY TALE

My team and I like to meet with clients at least annually to review their progress and make sure they are on target to meet their goals for a happy and well-funded retirement. Last year we welcomed a new couple as our clients—let's call them Bill and Barb. Bill is a technology consultant who consults with the federal government; Barb is a housewife. These two sixty-five-year-olds had never worked with a financial advisor before and had no retirement plan until they came to us—at sixty-four—hoping to retire soon.

But how? "We can barely get by on $120,000 a year," Bill said to me. And yet he still hoped he and his wife could waltz into their sunset years and leave the drudgery of work behind them.

Unfortunately, Bill and Barb had not saved during their working years and had very little in investments—just $250,000 in an individual retirement account (IRA) and $200,000 in home equity. To even *consider* retirement, they would need to become *aggressive savers*, meaning they needed to save much more than the standard 10 percent of their income per year.

Bill and Barb had a lot of catching up to do.

During our consultation, we asked them how much they thought various goods and services cost—for example, a new four-door sedan no longer costs $30,000, as it did ten years ago when they bought theirs. Today they are looking to replace their car with a $50,000 comparable vehicle. Property taxes have gone up 25 percent in the past ten years. Homeowner's insurance has gone up too. To enjoy a night at the movies today means shelling out $20 a ticket. Barb seemed truly shocked. "Whatever happened to the $5 or $6 movie?" I don't know what these two had been doing for the past decade, but the exercise was an eye-opener for them.

Though they didn't realize it, Bill and Barb were experiencing inflation. And as hard as it is to fathom, prices will double *again* between now and when they reach age ninety in just twenty-four years. It's that big bad Rule of 72 rearing its head again.

What's the lesson here? Be prepared or be disappointed. We'll revisit Bill and Barb in a future chapter to see how their finances shaped up.

## ANNIVERSARY REFLECTIONS

My wife and I were on a walk through our neighborhood one recent August afternoon and she mentioned it was our anniversary! I panicked at first, but then I became confused—we were married in September... right? It turned out she was referring to the twenty-third anniversary of the day we moved into our home. Relieved it wasn't our wedding anniversary, I began to think about inflation and compounding as it related to our home. (That's a guy thinking, I suppose.) Doing some quick calculations, I estimated our home had doubled in price since we'd purchased it—or increased at a rate of 3 percent per year. Initially I was surprised, but that growth reflects the average increase in the price of housing over a long period of time.

Look at figure 2.3. It illustrates how home prices have steadily increased in the past thirty years.

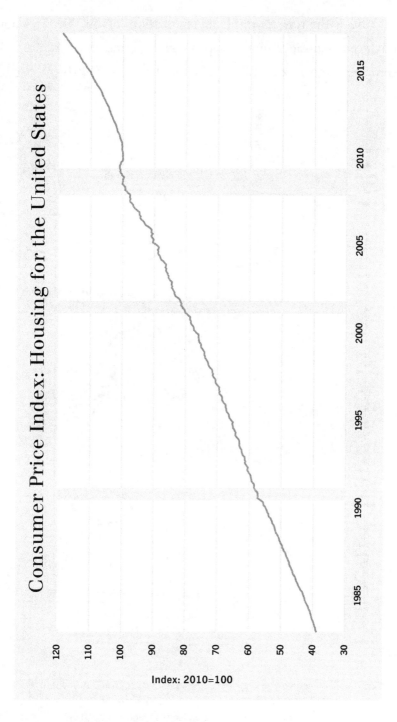

Figure 2.3 Source: FRED® Economic Data, accessed 2018.

*Now* is the time to think about inflation in your life. Still not convinced? Consider food—staples like beef and milk. Figure 2.4 represents a short view of food inflation, from 1992–2014:

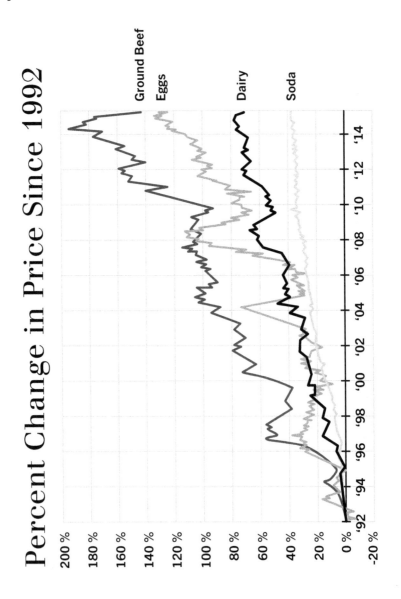

Figure 2.4 Source: Andy Kiersz, "Here's How the Price of Food Has Changed Since 1992," Business Insider, July 16, 2015, accessed 2018, https://www.businessinsider.com/food-inflation-chart-2015-7.

The bottom line: Inflation will be a factor over your lifetime and most assuredly during your retirement years, when you're most vulnerable to it. During that twenty- or thirty-year time frame, your income must grow, or your standard of living will decrease.

## OK, SO INFLATION IS OUT THERE. WHAT CAN I DO ABOUT IT?

My team and I believe that rather than burying your head in the sand, you need to own a *portfolio of companies* that grow their dividends at a rate *in excess of* the inflation rate. Over time, this will provide greater purchasing power for investors. We have no idea what the "value of the portfolio" will do, but an educated guess (and the entire history of the stock market) suggests that it will increase. Remember, you do not spend the value of your portfolio—you spend the *income* off the portfolio. How do we get there? By focusing on income, which we'll explore in the next chapter.

# CHAPTER THREE

# Focus on Income, Not Market Value

One of the oldest women of all time, Nabi Tajima of Japan, recently passed away at 117 years old. The matriarch presided over a family of 140 descendants—nine children, twenty-eight grandchildren, fifty-six great-grandchildren, and thirty-five great-great-grandchildren. Though it's unclear what she did during her working years to support her family, imagine if you were in her shoes. Imagine you worked for fifty solid years, then retired at age sixty-five, and lived for another fifty years—are you prepared for potentially *five* decades without earning a paycheck? Tajima's case may seem extreme, but with life expectancies ever increasing, it's not outside the realm of possibility that healthy, non-smoking Americans could live twenty, thirty, forty, and yes, even fifty years into their retirement.

This may be stating the obvious, but that's a long time, and it can feel even longer if you're nervous about funding it.

Think about your life beyond your finances. I'll bet there are other "banks" in your life that receive deposits. I can think of three very important banks: intellectual stimulation, emotional

31

happiness, and available resources. I believe the traditional definition of retirement—the one our culture and most of the Western World embraces—is bankrupt. It does *nothing* for these three banks that require regular deposits as well. Here's what I mean:

- INTELLECTUAL DEPOSITS mean you're figuring things out. You're involved in something that keeps your mind stimulated and engaged. Making this kind of an investment can be learning a new language, taking up a new activity or sport, or even acquiring a new skill. As Roman poet Juvenal said, "Mens sana in corpore sano." In other words, "Sound mind, sound body."

- EMOTIONAL DEPOSITS mean you're connected with a group or a team. This may sound cliché, but you can feel the love. An emotional deposit ensures your heart isn't neglected—you're visiting with loved ones regularly and/ or meeting new people.

- RESOURCE DEPOSITS refer to cash. You get benefits, perks, your parking spot, those sorts of things.

We *all* need deposits in those three bank accounts, and no one in the mainstream financial media is talking about it. Instead, most traditional retirement commercials promote the fiction that retirement is all about self-indulgent, endless vacations, filled with golf and endless rounds of frothy mixed drinks enjoyed by a sparkly pool.

Sorry everyone, but the "golden years" are bunk.

And yet the industry I work in promotes the stereotype. If you choose to spend your retirement the way slick advertising executives think you should, be my guest. But I have a feeling that kind of lifestyle becomes unfulfilling and—believe it or not—boring.

I think a modern retirement involves a balance between personal time, working for intellectual stimulation, and engagement in social activities. Discovering and striking a comfortable balance will be the most important endeavor for new retirees.

But sadly, even if most retirees want to invest in those areas of their lives, many just don't have the ability to do so. According to a study done by Bankrate.com, as many as 70 percent of Americans will not be able to freely make those choices. Instead, they will have to work "as long as possible" because they "need the money." The study also says that:

- 38 percent of respondents plan to work because they want to.

- 35 percent plan to work because they need the money.

- 27 percent plan to work because they need the money *and* want to work.

Additionally, 47 percent of retirees are either very worried or somewhat worried about outliving their retirement savings. That's *up* from 37 percent when the survey was last conducted in 2009. These are some sobering statistics, but I believe they could be different.

I value many freedoms, especially financial, emotional, and intellectual ones. My team and I specialize in creating financial freedom, and we encourage clients to prepare for retirement with all those freedoms in mind.

The best way to protect those freedoms when it comes to investing is to make sure that your income is growing and that you're spending *income,* not spending principal.

## CHANGING THE DEFINITION OF RETIREMENT

The definition of retirement is changing radically. Today, people entering this phase of their lives are closely examining the outcomes of those who walked the same path ten years ago. What happened to that group? Many decided that working on their golf game, bridge, or nothing at all is not a fulfilling way to spend these years.

Retirees face two possible outcomes: your money outlasts you, or you outlast your money. (See chapter one again to review this concept.) Life expectancies increase every year, increasing the odds of the second outcome. With the first scenario, you keep your independence, dignity, and freedom and can pass along a legacy. In the second scenario, you lose your freedom, much of your dignity, and your independence. Plus, in the second scenario, there is almost no chance to pass anything along to your loved ones or to causes you care about.

How do I know this? From more than three decades of experience working on behalf of hundreds of clients. I have watched clients attempt to make the focus of their retirement improving their golf or bridge game, or by trying to fill the time with never-ending vacations in beautiful locales. However, I do *not* believe we were made to be on vacation the last third of our lives. Imagine vacationing for thirty-five or forty years—same food, same people, same meaningless routine. It sounds less like fun and more like a prison sentence.

I believe the real definition—maybe the new definition—of retirement is *freedom*. Freedom to decide how you want to invest your time and energy. Dan Sullivan (a personal hero of mine) of Strategic Coach breaks it down this way:

- *Freedom from* the traditional demands we place on ourselves or one another.

- *Freedom to* invest or allocate your time the way you want. Where and how you want to invest your time should be entirely up to you and not dictated by your account statements.

- *Freedom to* pursue interests. What interests you? Maybe it is your vocation, maybe it is an *avocation*. Maybe it involves helping others.

- *Freedom in* relationships. Who do you want to do things with—family, friends, partners? You should have the freedom to be with those you love when you want to be.

My proposed new definition of retirement is so radical because culturally, everybody's taught to pay attention to the *value* of their investment portfolio. The reality will be repeated a dozen times in this book, and I'll keep repeating it: ***You don't spend the value of your portfolio. You don't spend what it's worth; you spend the income off the portfolio.*** This is why it is so important to focus on your *income*, not on the value. Looking at the balance on your statement creates an emotional reaction—you feel good if the value is higher than last month, and you feel bad if the value is down.

Get off that roller coaster and try this instead: Look at the income number on your statement. Measure your income versus the income from last month. Make sure your income is going up over time.

Unfortunately, society and advertising have most of us trained pretty well. We're indoctrinated to focus with razor-like precision on our portfolio value. The daily media chatter only reinforces that.

It really shouldn't be a surprise that the financial press is sponsored by financial product manufacturers and those that benefit from your trading. Think about it: Why do so many financial stories plant seeds of doubt? Is it because those journalists or television anchors really understand your situation and want you to win? Or is it to get you to change your portfolio, specifically buying what they are selling? Financial news outlets sensationalize market movements every hour of the day just to get you to watch three minutes of commercials five times an hour for products trying to subtly sell you on some product. It is *all* a game—but a lucrative one; otherwise, companies wouldn't spend millions on it. Remember, it's lucrative for *them*, but not necessarily for *you*.

Rarely do investors plan or expect to spend the value of their portfolio. The value happens to be what an account may be worth, at a moment in time, if you were to sell or convert to cash.

So why let short-term price fluctuations determine both your emotional state and your long-term goals? Instead, have your portfolio work for you—generating cash flow that grows faster than the inflation rate. Does it really matter what the value is on a day-to-day basis if you are not going to spend the balance? No.

## RISE ABOVE THE NOISE WITH A TRUSTED ADVISOR

If you're still with me, you're probably wondering how to keep your sanity during the financial media onslaught. The best way I know how to do it is to provide clients a written plan and an advisor to keep them on track. Sometimes it helps to have someone remind you that what you're doing is the right thing, especially when it seems like everyone else is going in the other direction. A good advisor will walk this journey with you—guiding, coaching, and advising you on your path.

I have observed most members of the financial services industry, from academics to product managers, distributors to advisors, believe that no matter what, investors need to have some of their portfolio allocated to fixed income. Though well intended as a hedge against fluctuations in portfolios, this belief leads to the loss of investor purchasing power, and I disagree with it.

I believe the true path toward financial freedom comes from focusing on the income generated by your portfolio, not the day-to-day value.

## DAN: A CONSTANT REMINDER

One of my clients, Dan, recently came to see me. He was concerned about a holding in his portfolio: a technology firm that transformed into a global consumer products company. That meant nearly everyone, everywhere, owns the products this company makes. To me this was great news, but Dan wanted to talk about "the market" and how it was not doing well with his portfolio. You see he was concerned that the market was wiggling, and he did not like the wiggling values every day. He pointed out that his real estate rentals were not fluctuating every day—a comparison he liked to make. I stressed his portfolio was not "the market" and explained that *he owns a portfolio of businesses*—businesses looking to solve problems by providing goods and services to consumers who see value in those products. Those companies make a good product, turn a good profit, and share a portion of their profits with the owners—like Dan! The unfair comparison of what a portfolio of companies does day to day versus the value of real estate is an incorrect comparison. I doubt you'd want your realtor calling every day to tell you whether your house has gone up or down in value. Fortunately, Dan trusts us and heeds our advice, but we seem to have this same conversation with him two or three times a year. Dan, like many of us, needs to be coached and reminded frequently.

## STAY FOCUSED, STAY THE COURSE

Rather than worry about the ups and downs of your portfolio value, stay healthy. Pay attention to your health, both physical and mental. Stay fit with exercise, and stimulate your brain by reading. Stay strong in your skills. Keep up with changes and innovations; learn new skills with technology, especially the developments being embraced in your industry. Keep strong in your career.

Remember that each of these areas contributes to a healthy and meaningful retirement. Staying healthy, wealthy, and sharp will give you freedom. The freedom to continue working if you desire, or to start a business, or volunteer with a nonprofit. Remain engaged, remain active, and who knows, maybe you'll be celebrating your 117th birthday, too!

It's all about perspective.

CHAPTER FOUR

# The How, or What Do I Do About It? Show Me!

I f this book were a one-on-one session with a client, this is the point where my clients would often say, "OK, Steve. This is all interesting, and I'm in. What do you advise?"

Excellent question! We'll explore that in this chapter.

If you've been paying attention, you'll remember that I think Warren Buffett practices sound investing, so why not follow the same principles he does? Like Buffett, I believe in investing in great global companies, ones that sell their products or services to people like you and me every single day, no matter what's going on in the markets. These companies make a profit on what they sell, pay dividends, and *increase* those dividends paid to the owners of the company.

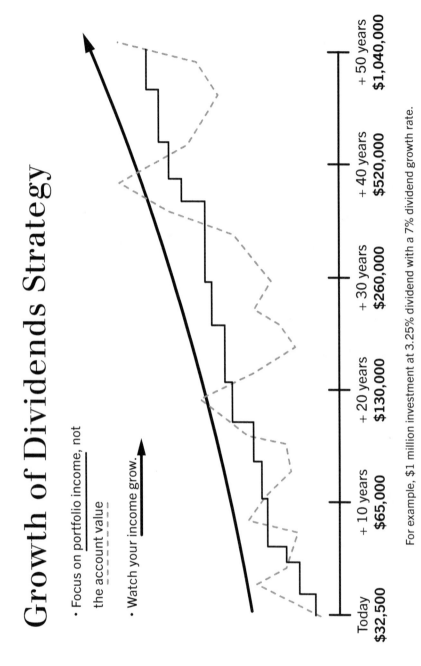

# Growth of Dividends Strategy

- Focus on portfolio income, not the account value

- Watch your income grow.

| | Today $32,500 | +10 years $65,000 | +20 years $130,000 | +30 years $260,000 | +40 years $520,000 | +50 years $1,040,000 |

For example, $1 million investment at 3.25% dividend with a 7% dividend growth rate.

Figure 4.1 This is a hypothetical example and is not representative of any specific investment. Your results may vary. The payment of dividends is not guaranteed. Companies may reduce or eliminate the payment of dividends at any time.

So, let's examine the Prosperion strategy. Take a look at figure 4.1. Notice the two lines: a black stepped line, and a gray jagged line. Both trend up and to the right, as indicated by the swooping arrow.

What exactly are we looking at? The stairstep. Dividends increase, then stay consistent until they increase again. The gray jagged line (the price, a.k.a. the emotion line) is the one all the talking heads get so excited about. As you can see there are fluctuations, but the general trend is an upward one, and that's the most important fact to remember. Focus on what the stair line is doing, not the jagged line—it's better for your sanity.

## THE ERROR OF EXTRAPOLATION

The error of extrapolation means we assume something will happen based on what we've most recently experienced and that the experience will continue indefinitely. For example, let's extrapolate the financial market we're in right now. Historically, the lack of volatility over the last two years is unprecedented. Markets typically go through some sort of a price correction, a short-lived dip of 10–15 percent, every twelve to sixteen months. That's normal.

This is where extrapolation can get you into trouble. People who extrapolate will say, "Well, markets don't correct anymore"—a huge mistake. The same thing happened with interest rates back in the 1970s. Interest rates were incredibly high—12 percent on a mortgage was normal. "Interest rates are never coming down," people said, and if the theory of extrapolation were correct, then interest rates today would be near 20 percent. But they're not. They're at historic lows.

Nothing is fixed in the financial markets, even though there's always a temptation to say that something will never change. People can be awfully forgetful—or dare I say lazy. I believe many people are just too lazy to think beyond what they expect to happen in the short term. I also think the media bear a lot of the blame here because they sensationalize any metric to get higher ratings. (More on that in chapter six.)

The first step toward progress requires honesty, recognition, and acceptance. Just as people are lazy in their diet and exercise habits, they're lazy in their financial ones, too. "I'll just sock some cash away and forget about it," some might say. That's OK as long as that person received solid advice and wasn't sold an unnecessary product. In that case, laziness has taken hold.

Don't be lazy—be willing to look beyond the here and now (see figures 4.2a, 4.2b, 4.3, and 4.4).

While we personally do not use the Dividend Aristocrats ETF, it is the most comparable ETF we are aware of that is currently available to the average investor and a good basis for comparison purposes.

# CONSISTENCY OF DIVIDEND COMPANIES

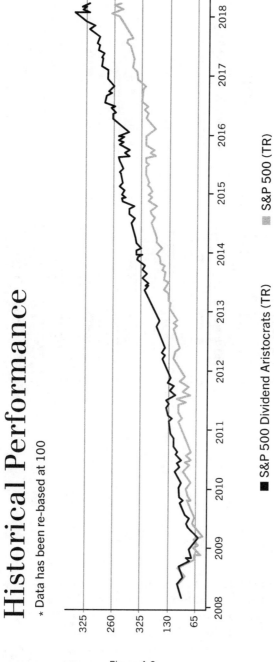

Figure 4.2a

43

# Performance of Dividend Aristocrats

| INDEX LEVEL | RETURNS | | | ANNUALIZED RETURNS | | | |
|---|---|---|---|---|---|---|---|
| | 1 MO | 3 MOS | YTD | 1 YR | 3 YRS | 5 YRS | 10 YRS |
| TOTAL RETURNS | | | | | | | |
| 2,408.94 | -0.92% | -2.24% | -2.24% | 13.30% | 10.07% | 12.82% | 12.42% |
| PRICE RETURNS | | | | | | | |
| 1,104.95 | -1.16% | -2.81% | -2.81% | 10.60% | 7.37% | 10.10% | 9.36% |
| NET TOTAL RETURNS | | | | | | | |
| 474.89 | -0.99% | -2.41% | -2.41% | 12.48% | 9.26% | 12.00% | 11.50% |
| BENCHMARK* TOTAL RETURNS | | | | | | | |
| 5,173.19 | -2.54% | -0.76% | -0.76% | 13.99% | 10.78% | 13.31% | 9.49% |
| BENCHMARK* PRICE RETURNS | | | | | | | |
| 2,640.87 | -2.69% | -1.22% | -1.22% | 11.77% | 8.49% | 10.97% | 7.16% |

Figure 4.2b

Figures 4.2a and 4.2b The S&P 500 Index is an unmanaged index, which cannot be invested into directly. Past performance is no guarantee of future results. Source: S&P Dow Jones Indices, S&P 500 Dividend Aristocrats, accessed 2018, https://us.spindices. com/indices/strategy/sp-500-dividend-aristocrats; Sure Dividend, "The 2018 Dividend Aristocrats List: 25+ Years of Rising Dividends," updated June 5, 2018, https://www suredividend.com/dividend-aristocrats-list/#history.

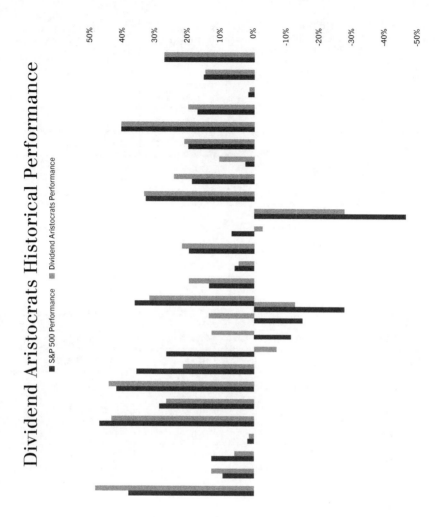

Figure 4.3 The performance of the Dividend Aristocrats by calendar year versus the S&P 500. The S&P 500 Dividend Aristocrats Index is an unmanaged index, which cannot be invested into directly. Past performance is no guarantee of future results. Source: Sure Dividend, "The 2018 Dividend Aristocrats List: 25+ Years of Rising Dividends," updated June 5, 2018, https://www.suredividend.com/dividend-aristocrats-list/#history.

| | DIVIDEND ARISTOCRATS PERFORMANCE | S&P 500 PERFORMANCE | RELATIVE PERFORMANCE |
|---|---|---|---|
| 1991 | 38.5 % | 30.5 % | 8.0 % |
| 1992 | 10.1 % | 7.6 % | 2.5 % |
| 1993 | 4.3 % | 10.1 % | -5.8 % |
| 1994 | 0.9 % | 1.4 % | -0.5 % |
| 1995 | 34.6 % | 37.6 % | -3.0 % |
| 1996 | 20.9 % | 23.0 % | -2.1 % |
| 1997 | 35.5 % | 33.4 % | 2.1 % |
| 1998 | 16.8 % | 28.6 % | -11.8 % |
| 1999 | -5.4 % | 21.0 % | -26.4 % |
| 2000 | 10.1 % | -9.1 % | 19.2 % |
| 2001 | 10.8 % | -11.9 % | 22.7 % |
| 2002 | -9.9 % | -22.1 % | 12.2 % |
| 2003 | 25.4 % | 28.7 % | -3.3 % |
| 2004 | 15.5 % | 10.9 % | 4.6 % |
| 2005 | 3.7 % | 4.9 % | -1.2 % |
| 2006 | 17.3 % | 15.8 % | 1.5 % |
| 2007 | -2.1 % | 5.5 % | -7.6 % |
| 2008 | -21.9 % | -37.0 % | 15.1 % |
| 2009 | 26.6 % | 26.5 % | 0.1 % |
| 2010 | 19.4 % | 15.1 % | 4.3 % |
| 2011 | 8.3 % | 2.1 % | 6.2 % |
| 2012 | 16.9 % | 16.0 % | 0.9 % |
| 2013 | 32.3 % | 32.4 % | -0.1 % |
| 2014 | 15.8 % | 13.7 % | 2.1 % |
| 2015 | 0.9 % | 1.4 % | -0.5 % |
| 2016 | 11.8 % | 12.0 % | -0.2 % |
| 2017 | 21.7 % | 21.8 | -0.1% |
| 1991-2017 | 12.9 % | 10.7 % | 2.1 % |

Figure 4.4 Past performance is no guarantee of future results. Source: Seeking Alpha, "The Dividend Aristocrats and Maximum Drawdowns," February 24, 2015, https://seekingalpha.com/article/2944126-the-dividend-aristocrats-and-maximum-drawdowns; Sure Dividend, "The 2018 Dividend Aristocrats List: 25+ Years of Rising Dividends," update June 5, 2018, https://www.suredividend.com/dividend-aristocrats-list/#history.

## WE LOVE GLOBAL COMPANIES

We love to invest in great global companies for three main reasons. One, we pick companies that make or distribute *products* people use every day around the world—name-brand soap, toothpaste, laundry detergent, cell phones. Two, we like companies that make a nice product *and* make a nice *profit* for their investors. If an investor sees a company having difficulty with its profits, and profits are where dividends come from, that investor may think twice about sticking with that company. Three, we look for companies that pay *dividends*.

The physical address or location of the corporate office is less important than the areas or regions of the world where the products or services are sold. Great companies sell their products to growing populations that, on average, move up the socioeconomic ladder—meaning the world population is growing into a larger population of consumers. What kinds of products do the global population consume? The same ones you and I buy—basics such as toilet paper, toothpaste, food, energy, communications, and computing products.

There are different types of companies that fit our three criteria:

One type is companies that make *consumable products.* These are items consumers buy regularly, which means they have an ongoing stream of sales. Often, those sales grow when new customers are introduced to the products.

A *wide moat* business is so big and beloved that it's difficult for rivals to gain market share. Think how difficult it would be to break into the men's shaving business, or the adhesive bandage business.

Why? Because the global leaders in those businesses have a tremendous advantage in how they manufacture, distribute, and sell their products. They have momentum that can only be broken by someone or some entity that disrupts the process of how a particular product is made—typically by making it faster and cheaper.

No matter the type of company, the primary purpose of a business is to make a *profit* by converting raw materials and resources into something of value to consumers. Stockholders make money when these profit-generating companies pay out *dividends*—a portion of the excess capital distributed to shareholders. This is getting paid while you wait—who wouldn't like that? It's usually a healthy sign when a company increases the dividend or distribution to the owners because it means management has confidence in the future. When dividend income increases at a rate equal to inflation, purchasing power remains steady. When the increase exceeds the inflation rate, you are earning more income, which in turn gives you the power to buy more goods and services in the future.

Remember, dividends are not guaranteed—they're paid out at the discretion of the board of directors—but by applying a little wisdom and understanding of the market, we can usually determine whether a company will perform well. We look for companies that have consistently paid and increased dividends over ten, twenty, or thirty years.

Take a company like Coca-Cola. Its dividend has grown every year for the last fifty-five years. There is no guarantee that will continue every year, but that's the trend. Procter & Gamble has paid a dividend for more than one hundred years straight. It's not guaranteed, but I'd call that a trend. A *trend* is different from *extrapolation;*

trends are based on long-term data. Extrapolation is when people only look at the recent past to determine future outcomes.[2]

Another great example is See's Candies. In 1972, the owners of See's approached the Oracle of Omaha himself, Warren Buffett, and asked him to buy the company. In 2007, See's Candies generated $383 million in pretax sales, with $82 million in profits. Buffett's holding company, Berkshire Hathaway, has earned $1.5 billion from that initial investment of $25 million back in 1972. So an initial investment of $25 million in 1972 now generates more than $100 million per year.[3]

What makes See's different from Hershey's? The profit margin on See's chocolate is higher than on a Hershey bar. Hershey's is more of a commodity business—it can't charge a high price because it's just Hershey's chocolate—but See's can charge a premium because it is a premium brand. The brand is held in high esteem by the public because its chocolate is known to be high quality, and the high price enables the owners to enjoy a wider profit margin. Wider profit margins mean more capital to return to the shareholders and owners and more opportunity to reinvest in the business.

## DIVIDEND-PAYING COMPANIES AREN'T PERFECT

Sometimes great companies do stupid things. General Electric is a prime example. The company had a solid track record of paying dividends every year from 1899 on. In 2008, during the global

---

2   All companies and securities mentioned in this book are examples only and not specific recommendations. Seek the help of a financial advisor when selecting securities for your specific situation.

3   Patrick Morris, "Warren Buffett bought this company for $25 million. Now it makes nearly $100 million every year," *Motley Fool*, July 13, 2014, https://www.fool.com/investing/general/2014/07/13/warren-buffett-bought-this-company-for-25-million.aspx.

financial crisis, General Electric had to cut its dividend because although it's not a bank, one of its divisions is GE Capital, which was deemed to be too big to fail.

Eventually GE turned around and, by 2010, began to raise its dividend. At the time we believed the dividend cut was not self-inflicted; it was imposed by regulators. Maybe GE was back on track again, now that it had returned to raising the dividend on a regular basis? But GE's board got out a little over its skis and had to cut the dividend again in 2017. This time it *was* self-inflicted. Why? Because GE was paying out more than what it really could afford while also trying to reinvest in the business.

What did we do? We sold GE shares because these actions undercut the very reason we invested in it in the first place—for the income. They cut the dividend, we sold our shares.

Smart investors look for income today, or income tomorrow. Most people think of companies and only consider appreciation. Yes, investments do appreciate if companies grow their sales, earnings, and business. But investing in *dividend-paying companies* is one of the most consistent forms of investment income, which sounds counter-intuitive. Stock prices can be volatile, but the cash flows from those companies collectively do not fluctuate as much as you might think.

The reason dividend investing is not highly publicized is because it's not sexy. Dividends are about as exciting as watching paint dry. It's not profitable for Wall Street because Wall Street doesn't make money on people who hold their investments. Wall Street profits when people transact. Media coverage of the financial markets creates doubt, which then creates comparison, which then causes people to say, "Maybe I should sell my Coca-Cola shares and invest in something else." Then people get off track. Simple dividends are not as profitable as other products Wall Street would rather sell, like mutual funds and annuities, which generate billions of dollars for them but may not be in investors' best interest.

Remember, most big public companies are in business to profit. I'm not writing this to make people happy. I'm just being brutally honest.

According to research by Yale's Robert Shiller, from September 1929 to June 1932, stock prices fell 81 percent, yet dividends fell only 11 percent. That means that during the worst financial disaster the United States has ever experienced, dividends were cut only a bit more than 10 percent. People still made money.

The Depression wasn't the only time this happened. In the bear market of 1973–1974, stock prices fell 54 percent, and dividends fell just 6 percent. In the 2000–2002 bear market, prices fell 50 percent, while dividends dropped just 2 percent. And in the most recent bear market of 2007–2009, dividends actually *rose* slightly, until six months after 2009 when the federal government forced banks to suspend paying dividends. This move caused dividends to decline 19 percent.

Take a look at the long-term historical data Shiller provides for dividend growth over the past seven decades. This shows the rolling twelve-month growth rates over one, three, and five years for dividends on the S&P 500, how often they were positive, and by how much.

| TIME FRAME | POSITIVE PERIODS | NEGATIVE PERIODS | AVERAGE |
|:---:|:---:|:---:|:---:|
| 1 YEAR | 87 % | 13 % | 5.8 % |
| 3 YEARS | 89 % | 11 % | 19.8 % |
| 5 YEARS | 100 % | 0 % | 33.9 % |

Figure 4.5  Source: Robert Shiller data available via Yale.edu.

Dividends are not guaranteed, but rarely do they fall. And when they do fall, they do not fall nearly as much as the market. Since 1945, dividends have increased by a factor of sixty-five.

Looking back at investments in the S&P 500, you would observe a stable cash flow that increased faster than inflation. In figure 4.6, take a look at the growth rates through the decades:

| DECADE | TOTAL GROWTH | ANNUAL GROWTH | INFLATION RATE |
|--------|--------------|---------------|----------------|
| 1950 | 60.5 % | 4.8 % | 2 % |
| 1960 | 72.7 % | 5.6 % | 2.3 % |
| 1970 | 95.6 % | 6 % | 7.1 % |
| 1980 | 95.6 % | 6.9 % | 5.5 % |
| 1990 | 49.1 % | 4.1 % | 3 % |
| 2000 | 36 % | 3.1 % | 2.6 % |
| 2010 | 93.6 % | 6.8 % | 1.7 % |

Figure 4.6 Past performance is no guarantee of future results. Source: Robert Shiller data available via Yale.edu.

Apart from the 1970s, each decade saw dividend growth outpace inflation. Such historical facts seem lost in the minds of most investors, which goes to show how powerful the financial media juggernaut really is in influencing investors' emotions.

It's hard to look at these charts and not agree with what they're showing. The problem occurs when cash flow is rising while prices are temporarily declining, which makes it hard for investors to remain calm. This is when investment advisors earn their keep.

Companies that raise dividends show confidence in the growth prospects of their business, their team, and their company.

## MY STARBUCKS STORY

In 1998, I wanted to teach my two sons, ages three and seven at the time, about investing and capitalism. Looking for an example, I went to a consumer products company my children were already familiar with: Starbucks. This company specialized in coffee, yet it was different because it was trying to create a community where people could gather and socialize.

Both of our boys were familiar with Starbucks and their delicious Frappuccinos. That evening, I brought home a Starbucks research report from Valueline and slipped it under my dinner table placemat. During dinner, I mentioned we were getting a refund on our taxes and wanted the family's input on where we might invest. I suggested buying one of these coffee shops.

I helped my sons to understand profit: the difference between what it costs to make their drink and what that drink sold for. Then I asked them to think about all the people we routinely saw coming and going from this little coffee shop. We realized we could end up with a pretty sweet little business. They were excited about the idea of making money until I mentioned we would need to take care of the shop, clean the bathrooms, load the snowblower in the Suburban to make sure people could get in the front door on snowy days, and so on. Suddenly the excitement vanished. I reached under the placemat to show them the report, and we talked about not owning just one but a piece of thousands of locations. That rekindled their excitement. Then I mentioned their labor participation in the investment: opening an envelope monthly to see how the company was doing. Our cost basis was around $2.60 per share (about the price of a Frappuccino back then). Today (in 2018), company shares run around $60—twenty-three times higher.

Starbucks did not pay dividends back in 1998, but today its annual dividend equals about the same dollar amount we invested.

That, dear readers, is growth of income.

CHAPTER FIVE

# Show Me More

Every day some companies focus on doing what they do in a way that's faster, quicker, easier, better, and cheaper than their equally eager competitors. These firms are constantly striving to add more value for consumers, their clients, and their local economies. This is how organizations go from good to great, and these are the types of companies my team and I look for as investments.

## KNOWLEDGE + DATA = WISDOM

So much information is readily available that you may be thinking, "Why can't I just do this myself?"

Data on its own is useless.

Data coupled with industry knowledge is *wisdom*. Knowledge means being able to *interpret the data* and, through judicious application of perspective and judgment, to make a calculated decision about what to do with specific investments.

Sure, you can automate data—the internet is proof of that. But you can't automate wisdom.

55

I can automate purchasing goods through Amazon, but I can't automate the relationship I have with my tailor, who knows my specific needs, desires, and wants—what I want my shirts to look like when I put them on.

*That's* wisdom.

When I visit my tailor I am expecting him to use the tools of his trade to make something that fits me like a glove. The same principle applies to examining financial data. There's never been so much information available to us, but it's *what you do* with data—how you apply it—that equals true wisdom, and that's why you go to an expert.


## HOW WE EVALUATE A COMPANY

When my team and I evaluate a company for our clients, we follow a specific set of guidelines to help us determine whether a company is a solid choice. First, we determine what the company does. Is it a company we are familiar with, one whose products or services we can easily recognize?

Next, we generally look for stable companies with great track records. We're not interested in investing clients' money in unknown, untested start-ups. Companies often exhibit specific traits and characteristics signaling to us they're worth investing in. Specifically, these companies provide essential products and services—things like toilet paper, toothpaste, and Wi-Fi. A company that only makes lipstick is not producing an essential product or service.

My team and I look for companies run by honest management teams who understand they are working for the owners and shareholders of the company. These CEOs are good stewards of their companies and their bottom lines. Our top picks are consistently profitable, even in economic downturns, and consistently pay a portion of corporate profits to shareholders and owners in the form of dividends. These companies also pay off their debts in a timely manner.

Finally, we invest in companies that typically buy back shares when prices reflect a good value, such as when the stock price is low relative to historic values or relative to the current price-to-earnings ratio. That's it, in a nutshell. If companies don't meet these criteria, we don't invest.

Let's delve a little deeper into each of these characteristics so you understand our thinking. Take Walmart as an example.

As I mentioned earlier, my team and I love companies that provide *essential* products and services, and for the most part, Walmart fits the bill. When Sam Walton took Walmart public in the 1980s, there were *6 billion* shares available. His children—Rob, Jim, and Alice Walton—have not sold any of his stock, but through stock buybacks the company is returning larger dividends to their shareholders.

Here's how: When Walmart went public, each of his children owned about 8 percent of the company. Today, they own upwards of 16 percent of the company because Walmart has shrunk the number of outstanding shares. How could that happen? If a company is generating cash, there are a few things it can do. First, the company must pay taxes. Then it pays employees. Finally, the company pays its shareholders in the form of a dividend. Whatever is left over is retained earnings.

Walmart's got to do something with those retained earnings. They could open Super Walmarts, neighborhood stores, or experiment with online and delivery platforms. Walmart has done all these things and still has money left over.

What to do? Walmart's executives may look at their company and say, "Hey, the historic price of our company has been *twenty times* earnings." That's a formula called the *price-to-earnings ratio*. If there is too much money left over, maintaining that ratio requires some action. Walmart has several choices:

- Give the excess to shareholders in the form of a large dividend; or

- Be prudent and buy back stock while it's selling at a discount compared to what it sells at historically.

Walmart has historically chosen to buy back shares when faced with the question of what to do with excess capital. That's how the Walton children each now own approximately 16 percent of the company—they shrunk the number of outstanding shares on the market.

From a shareholder perspective, if somebody wants to buy a piece of Walmart they can, but the price has gone up because there are fewer outstanding shares available for purchase. That also means each share is worth more, so the investment will likely be a smart choice.

The price of Walmart is just a data point—it's what shares would trade for today. The question is whether the price is too high or too low. It takes wisdom to understand the data point (price) relative to every price it ever has been, or ever could be.

Let's look at the flip side. Let's say the Walton children like the company and each owns 8 percent of Walmart. Rather than buying back stock, the company issues more. When executives are awarded stock options and grants, they are getting shares of the company. It's like a paycheck—the currency just happens to be shares of Walmart rather than Benjamin Franklins. This increases the number of shares outstanding. If the Waltons own 8 percent of the company and the total number of shares doubles from 4 billion to 8 billion, they now own 4 percent. This process is known as *dilution*.

Dilution doesn't sound very good, does it? It depends on other factors at play. Ultimately it's all about allocating resources appropriately and to the benefit of shareholders. My team and I are happy if a company makes a dollar in profit, after taxes, and pays a portion of it to shareholders in the form of a dividend.

Guess what? Even though we love Walmart, it is *not* in our portfolio. Why? Walmart has nearly tripled sales in the last fifteen years. That's wonderful. They are kicking butt and taking names. Yet, even after explaining all the great ways Walmart rewards its stockholders, we don't invest in it. So, when clients come in and ask why we don't invest in Walmart, we talk about how we manage our portfolio.

Let's look at that now.


## PORTFOLIO MANAGEMENT USING QUALITATIVE KNOWLEDGE

Let's continue using Walmart as our example. In my opinion, retail is cyclical and hard—just look at how Amazon is disrupting retail. Even though the data says Walmart is doing great, my team and I have the wisdom to look at the whole picture and see retail is a tough place to be right now, no matter how good a company looks on paper.

*Qualitative knowledge* requires understanding the direction a company is going, where its competitors are, and applying that knowledge to the current business. In the case of Walmart, I'd rather not take the risk. I'd rather use the same capital to invest in Johnson & Johnson. Johnson & Johnson products are sold at Walmart and they're also sold on Amazon. Amazon cannot squeeze the price of Band-Aid® brand adhesive bandages, which are made by Johnson & Johnson. Amazon and Walmart are just distributors. I prefer to own stock in the companies *making* products people buy, not companies *selling* products people buy.

When we're considering whether to invest in a company, one of the first things we determine is whether the company is fairly valued. The current price of a stock is easy to determine—it is available everywhere we have the internet, from nearly every digital device. My son gets prices on his watch. Stock prices are as readily available as the time right now. But it's just data. The real challenge is understanding the worth of a company and evaluating the value against the price. Investors look for a discrepancy between the two, with a lower price relative to the economic value as the best situation.

How do you determine the worth of a company? When buying shares, you are investing in a *portion of the company as it is today*. You are buying a percentage of the property, warehouses, locations, patents, intellectual property, inventory, and cash on the balance sheet and in the bank. You are also buying a portion of the company's debt and liabilities. All these things factor into *book value*, or an accounting of what the company is claiming to be worth for accounting purposes.

Here's an example of book value: Let's say you own a piece of rental property. You can depreciate it over a twenty-year period. You can't depreciate your own house because you use it, but you can depreciate a rental. You can deduct one-twentieth of the home's value over twenty years, and deduct that against the rental income, so they wash each other out. When you go to sell the property at year twenty, your cost basis is zero. You must pay taxes on the price versus your cost basis.

Tax laws permit companies to depreciate the value of assets on their books. So, for accounting purposes, a company may have an asset on the books for $500, yet it may be worth $1,000 on the open market. Understanding these discrepancies takes persistence and a willingness to ask questions.

Smart investors also focus on a company's future income stream. Forecasting earnings is difficult, but someone like me has the knowledge to look at company revenue histories and build a good case for continued earnings. Think about consumer products companies, which we tend to favor. They sell goods to consumers, year in and year out. There is little volatility in their earnings because nearly everyone buys adhesive bandages, soap, bleach, and toothpaste.

Examining earnings is an art, but mastering it can give you confidence you are buying a company at a good value relative to its historical price-to-earnings ratio. The key is not to overpay. I believe you make all your money on the buy—meaning how good of an investment you make depends heavily on how low of a price you paid.

## CHARACTERISTICS OF SOLID INVESTMENTS

*Dividend yield* is one measure of the return to shareholders. Mathematically, the dividend rate is the current amount per share paid out to investors over an annual period divided by the current price. Dividends are typically paid to shareholders quarterly (see figure 5.1).

$$\text{Dividend Yield} = \frac{\text{Annual Dividend}}{\text{Current Stock Price}}$$

Figure 5.1

For example, if stock *XYZ* had a share price of $50 and an annualized dividend of $1.00, its yield would be 2 percent.

$1.00 / $50 = 0.02

When the 0.02 is put into percentage terms, it would make a 2 percent yield. If this share price rose to $60, but the dividend was not increased, its yield would fall to 1.66 percent.

Industries can follow dividend yield patterns. For example, power utilities tend to have a higher dividend yield as the growth of dividends and revenue for those companies tends to be slow. Growth in utilities depends on new customers, new homes, and other factors. Utilities are regulated by the government, which reviews and controls utility rates and subsequently what the utilities pay to shareholders in dividends. Our preference is to shy away from highly regulated industries and companies, and favor those that are more innovative. Consumer products companies also tend to produce healthier growth in revenue and dividends.

Some investors look solely at the dividend rate and do not understand the key to the dividend growth rate—in other words, the rate at which their future income will increase. That's shortsighted.

Here's what we consider a smart approach: Invest for income today or income in the future and look for dividends growing at a rate greater than inflation. Investments meeting these two criteria provide investors with *rising purchasing power*, irrespective of the price per share.

Higher-growth companies tend to have a lower dividend yield, meaning you may start out with a small dividend relative to the price per share. But let's imagine a company increases its dividend 20 percent annually. In that case, it only takes three-and-one-half years for the income to double from that investment. As you can see in figure 5.2, the dividend amount can grow to be significant to shareholders in a short time.

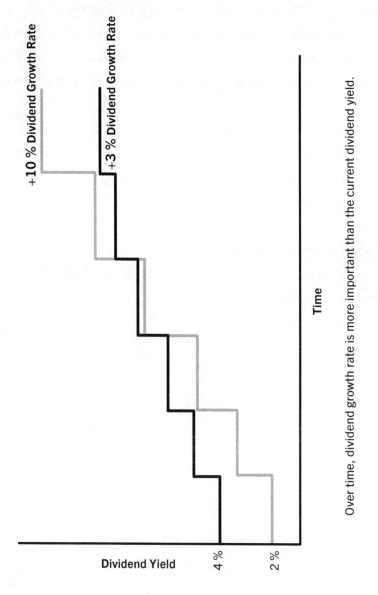

Figure 5.2 This is a hypothetical example and is not representative of any specific investment. Your results may vary.

We like companies that pay a nice dividend income today and demonstrate the ability to grow the dividend at a multiple of the inflation rate. By doing this, we attempt to double the income to our investors over a seven-to-ten-year time frame. If your income is doubling every seven to ten years, the purchasing power of your investments is increasing. That means more income and growing income during your retirement years.

Figure 5.3 is an example of what this looks like, comparing two dividend companies, one that pays a higher current dividend rate, four percent, but grows the dividend at three percent per year versus a company that starts out at a lower rate, two-and-one-half percent, but grows at eight percent. You start with a lower initial income, but as you can see from this illustration, over time (and especially over a typical retiree time frame) the faster the dividend growth rate, the better the investment.

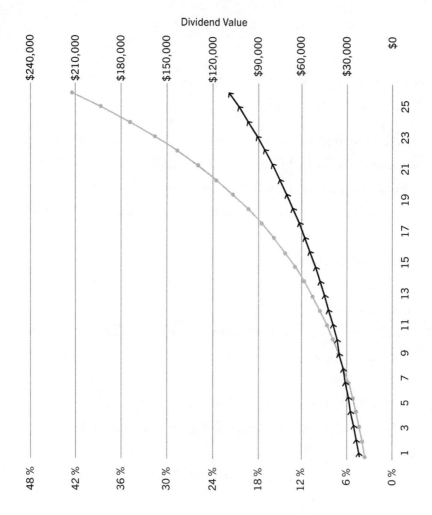

Figure 5.3 This is a hypothetical example and is not representative of any specific investment. Your results may vary. Source: Miller Howard Investments, Income Yield on Original Investment Calculator, accessed 2018, https://tools.mhinvest.com/mhichart.

That has a nice ring to it, don't you think?

## MY BERKSHIRE HATHAWAY STORY: THANK YOU, DOLORES

Dolores was one of my very first clients and a secretary for the Colorado Chamber of Commerce. One day back in 1980, Dolores called and asked me to purchase two shares of a company called Berkshire Hathaway. I was unsure what the company did, but based on the name I assumed they were in the shirt business—I had some Hathaway dress shirts.

After looking up the symbol and the price, I was surprised to see it trading around $750 per share. I called Dolores.

"Dolores, who would buy a stock at such a high price?" I asked. "That's an insane amount of money!"

"Steve, just buy it."

"But Dolores, *any* stock at that price is overpriced!"

She politely asked me again to buy her two shares, and finally, I obliged.

Fast-forward a couple of years, and Dolores called again, asking me to purchase another two shares of Berkshire Hathaway. Now the company was priced at $1,500 a share. We started going back and forth again and she reminded me of our prior conversation, so I obliged, adding two more shares to her account.

*Dolores must know something I don't*, I thought. Curiosity got to me when I saw this shirt maker was also a shareholder in GEICO, an auto insurer. Another client of mine worked at GEICO, so I called and asked if he knew anything about Berkshire Hathaway being a shareholder of GEICO. He had heard about this fellow, Warren Buffett, who was the owner. I started studying the company trying to figure out why a textile company would be investing in an auto insurance company.

Following the company for the next few years prompted me to begin investing in the shares. Today, Berkshire Hathaway is our largest holding. The share price has soared from $4,500 to more than $330,000, or about *seventy times* our initial investment.

I learned my lesson. I had to bone up on companies like Berkshire Hathaway early to act in my clients' best interests. That wasn't exactly standard practice thirty years ago: our industry has evolved from providing brokerage services to serving a fiduciary function, and that's a good thing. In a brokerage relationship, the only thing a stockbroker must do is determine if the investment is suitable. It doesn't mean the investment is good for the client; it just means the investment is *suitable*.

Today, we perform an advisory function. This means we've gone from determining whether a product is simply suitable to whether it's in the best interest of the client. We put the client's interest ahead of our own. Every day I'm researching each of these companies so I can understand them and know why our clients should own their stock. When you're a fiduciary, you pay attention to the details.

I don't enjoy reading about Walmart because it's cool. I hardly go into a Walmart, except to look around and see what they're doing—a little research and development.

Know what you own, and why you own it. Thank you, Dolores.

CHAPTER SIX

# Distractions

The media is competing for your mind *and* your money. I believe there's an unspoken agreement between advertisers, media, and the financial services industry to get people to spend money for products they might not really need.

Look, the financial services industry is incentivized to attract money and to trade money. That means financial services providers profit when money is in motion, so those providers will use every tool possible to attract money to themselves. As a result, their advertising is incredibly effective. How? By planting little seeds of doubt:

*Does your portfolio look like this?*

*Don't you wish your portfolio had this in it?*

*You have enough money for retirement—don't you?*

And so on.

Think about the last advertisement you saw for a financial company. Most likely, it suggested that what you have isn't enough.

Consider corporate sponsors of financial television shows on cable and business networks. All of them are selling products, but they're not selling soap; they're selling *financial* products. Make a mental note to focus on the commercials the next time you flip on CNBC or Fox Business. You're going to find mutual fund companies and money managers make up the bulk of advertising.

## TUNE OUT THE TALKING HEADS

Or better yet, maybe you should just forget about tuning in to your favorite business news program. I'm confident you'll feel better if you tune out the talking heads. Why? They're not doing you any favors; they're only trying to make money off your insecurities. Here's how: First, networks put together a business show in which the host does everything possible to get the viewer to feel insecure. Then comes the financial commercial saying, "Hey, I'm your answer!" That combination triggers purchasing behavior. It's slick and incredibly effective. Practically nobody with their own cable show is interested in your financial well-being. They're only interested in lining their pockets with product endorsements and advertising revenue.

Not enough proof for you? You don't have to take my word for it, take a look at Jim Cramer, the stock-picking pundit. His picks have been statistically debunked by a retired finance professor. In April 2016, David England tested Cramer's forty-nine top stock picks to see if they lived up to Cramer's exhortation that they must be part of any well-structured portfolio. England purchased $1,000 of each Cramer-recommended security. Then he tracked their performance over six months.

Guess what? Only *fourteen* of Cramer's forty-nine stocks closed higher after a period of market volatility.

Imagine how many people follow Cramer's advice and invest in his picks every day. Why wouldn't they? He's on television, so he *must* be an expert. But Cramer's main priority is to increase his show's ratings. A lot of people trust him, but I think he's only in the game to get rich.

What should you do instead? Turn off the television. I assure you, Warren Buffett does *not* watch CNBC or Fox Business. He doesn't have a computer in his office either. He reads the newspaper. Why? Because it is recent enough. Price only matters on two days: the day you buy and the day you sell. All the rest is noise.

Yet noise blurs the line between advertising and news, which negatively impacts investor behavior. One of the goals of this book is to *improve* investor outcomes by improving investor behavior. Turning off the TV is a smart step in the right direction.

There is a major disconnect between investor *experience* (i.e., how well investors perform) and mutual fund *performance*. Research firm DALBAR's most recent annual quantitative analysis of investor behavior concludes investors *do not experience the same investment return as the investments they own.* DALBAR found the average equity fund investor in the S&P 500 underperformed by 3.66 percent. And when the market gained as little as 1 percent, the average equity investor lost more than 2.28 percent.

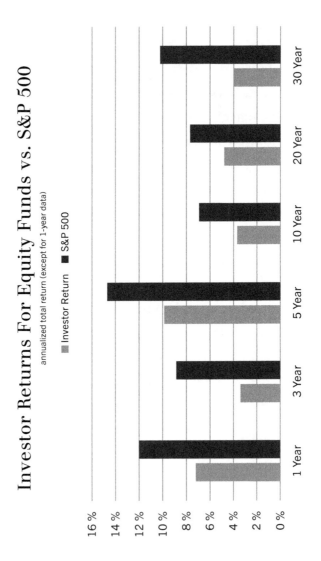

Figure 6.1 The S&P 500 Index is an unmanaged index, which cannot be invested into directly. Past performance is no guarantee of future results. DALBAR uses data from the Investment Company Institute (ICI), Standard & Poor's, Bloomberg Barclays Indices, and proprietary sources to compare mutual fund investor returns to an appropriate set of benchmarks. The study utilizes mutual fund sales, redemptions and exchanges each month as the measure of investor behavior. These behaviors reflect the "average investor." Based on this behavior, the analysis calculates the "average investor return" for various periods. These results are then compared to the returns of respective indexes. Ending values for the indexes and hypothetical equity investor investments are based on average annual total returns. Source: DALBAR, 24th Annual Quantitative Analysis of Investor Behavior, accessed 2018.

Those statistics raise the following question: Why would investors have a significantly lower return experience than what the fund delivered? It comes down to investor behavior (see figure 6.1). Investors buy after markets go up, and they sell after markets go down. The result is lower performance than the actual funds owned. The emotion involved in determining investor behavior can be an investor's worst enemy—and those talking heads on television are doing nothing but fueling poor, emotionally charged decisions.

Another major problem with our industry is payment for *activity* (i.e., transaction costs). This encourages buying and selling, whether it's necessary or not. Another problem is the complex products available, essentially allowing investors to "gamble" on the market using high amounts of leverage. I think this contributes to the quick market moves we've seen lately.

In recent years there has been an absence of volatility. That's amazing, because historically a sizeable drop occurs every eighteen months on average. It is the *lack of volatility* that is abnormal. It is *normal* for the markets to experience a short-term decrease in prices, which is typically followed by a long-term advance. If volatility is normal, what is abnormal is the speed with which the jumps in prices occur.

## BARRIERS COME DOWN AND SO DO PROTECTIONS

Some of you may recall Oliver Stone's 1987 drama *Wall Street*, where unscrupulous corporate raider Gordon Gekko represents all that is bad and unethical about capitalist trading. Yet watching the movie today feels so antiquated; the brokers had to enter tickets manually and be physically present on the trading floor to get anything done. Nowadays, anyone can get on his or her phone and in two seconds buy or sell millions of shares. Without barriers it's easy to get jumpy, and the media plays to those fears.

What are investors supposed to do if they can't trust what they see on TV? Everyone needs to have a plan. The one I encourage clients to use is called the Five Cs, based on Dan Sullivan's "4 C's Formula®."

Adding on to Dan's original formula, the first C is for *clarity.* It means you need to be clear about what it is that you want when it comes to retirement.

The second C stands for *commitment.* Commit to someone, like an advisor. Then make sure that advisor commits to *you.*

The third C is *courage.* You need *courage* to invest. Have the courage to step forward and make a change for the better.

The fourth C is *capability.* The capability of looking back and seeing what you have accomplished.

The final C is *confidence.* Be confident in the plan you've put together and in the path you're charting for yourself.

Lather, rinse, repeat. The Five Cs apply to both finance and everyday life.

Don't believe me? Here's what the Five Cs look like in a non-financial situation:

Let's say we're out skiing. (In addition to my financial practice, I also work as a part-time private ski instructor.) Everyone's coming from a different starting point: Some clients have never been on skis. Others haven't been on a hill in five years. And still others are facing the mountain after having their ACL repaired.

The first thing we do is talk and gain *clarity* on what those clients want to achieve during their outing.

Next, we develop a game plan. Why? Because we're going to *commit* to our game plan. Our game plan always has exits in case somebody gets injured. Then we *commit* to each other about what we're going to do.

Then we have the *courage* to start down the hill. When we get to the bottom, we look back up and realize, *Oh. That wasn't so hard. I actually can do this.* That's being *capable,* and the feeling of accomplishment fosters *confidence.*

Lather, rinse, repeat.

The same principles for learning to ski apply to investing.

First, you become *clear* about what you want, then you develop a game plan. We *commit* to each other, and then have the *courage* to invest. Both parties can accomplish what they need to do, and then, once the investment is completed, we look back and realize just how well we did, which makes us realize that we are *capable*—and that gives everyone tremendous *confidence.*

## MEET AL

Al retired from the National Renewable Energy Laboratory (NREL) based in Golden, Colorado. NREL is filled with engineers who figure out how to create energy from fans, the sun, and other renewable sources. Before he retired, Al used to be a hand-wringing type of person. Any time the market moved even a little bit, he would call us, his nervousness emanating from the phone. Even though my team developed the most incredible financial plan for him, Al always took our Excel spreadsheets and made them better. I could tell ten years out when Al was going to replace his car, because it was in his spreadsheet. *That's* how detail-oriented he was.

Meanwhile, Lynn, Al's wife, worked for the local Veterans Administration. She was always super calm because she knew that

Al would be watching over things. I believe she also had a lot of confidence in me.

"Are we going to be OK?" Lynn would ask.

"Yes," I always replied.

"OK, next topic. How are you and Marie doing? How are your kids?"

That was Lynn.

Al retired four years ago. He and Linda sold their house and moved down to New Mexico. Now Al's got little projects, and overall, he is having the time of his life. I don't hear from Al much anymore because he is retired and everything is *going to plan.* He's actually *ahead* of his plan in terms of how his assets are performing. He's got excess cash flow. As you can probably imagine, Al is very happy.

Recently, I called Al.

"Al, did you see the SpaceX rocket launch?" Being that he was an engineer, I thought he would really get into that.

"No," Al replied.

"Really?"

"That's right," Al said. "I don't watch any news. I am so much happier now that I don't watch any news."

"Well, let me tempt you," I said. "Go to YouTube and watch the Falcon Heavy launch, just for engineering's sake."

I don't know whether Al watched the launch or not, but the point is he learned to let go. Al learned to *turn off the news,* and he's happier for it.

Timothy Ferriss, in his landmark publication *The 4-Hour Workweek,* says we should stop watching news *completely.* Ferris suggests most people within a society believe it's our job to be well-informed, which means we must consume a massive amount of media. But with a twenty-four-hour news cycle, Ferris says we're killing ourselves instead. If you let go of the need to follow CNN ad nauseam, and on occasion must ask friends what's going on in the world, you're going to feel better about yourself and have a better grip on reality. When you only follow the big news items, you're not stressing over the minutiae of what passes for daily news.

I attempt to practice this approach and try not to watch more than forty minutes of television a night. By recording the news I can get through both the local and national headlines without commercials. Then I turn the television *off*. That takes discipline. I've passed on that dedication and discipline to my family members. Now they don't allow distraction in their lives, and they don't get whipped around.

Building discipline is like building a muscle. Initially, the work is hard. Developing discipline and setting up goals, time frames, and a strategy—then sticking to that strategy—has tangible benefits. I hope the examples throughout this book have demonstrated this. If you stay the course, there are great rewards to be enjoyed that go far beyond financial security.

How do you develop that stamina and discipline? We cover it all in the next chapter.

CHAPTER SEVEN

# Let's Talk About Implementation

I mplementation is about putting together a cohesive plan for my clients. In this chapter I'd like to walk you through what typical new clients go through when they sit down and meet with my team for the first time.

It all starts with one question to identify their goals, The Dan Sullivan Question[4]: "If we are meeting here three years from today, what needs to happen for you to be happy with your progress?" In other words, looking three years into the future, what would it take to make that client happy?

You may be thinking, "Why worry about a three-year plan in retirement?" A three-year period gives us a way to develop and work toward concrete goals. If clients are coming to us at age sixty-five holding a retirement check, that is a scary moment. That's their future.

---

4    Credit to Dan Sullivan, cofounder of Strategic Coach® (www.strategiccoach.com), a firm dedicated to coaching entrepreneurs worldwide. Dan has been my coach since 1999 and has fundamentally transformed my business and my life.

It's hard for people to sit down and describe what they want their lives to be like in ten or twenty years. We don't know what's going to happen five years from now. But three years out is achievable—you can practically reach out and touch it. One year is too short. Five years is kind of long. Three years feels about right.

We've thought long and hard about the phrasing of the question, too. People can generally visualize being happy three years from now. I want people to be *happy*, not just *satisfied*. To me, happiness is an emotional step above satisfaction. I'm not looking for satisfactory; I'm looking for *excellent*. And when you experience something excellent, you're happy about it.

We help our clients focus on their progress. A focus on progress is a look at what you've accomplished. If you focus on being perfect, you'll never be satisfied. It's like wishing for a perfect body. You'll never have a perfect body, but if you are five pounds overweight and you get it down to one pound or two pounds, you've made *progress*, and we must remain mindful of that progress. Progress is positive. Perfection is negative. Perfection creates negativity.

Sometimes we get a client who doesn't know how to answer the three-year question. It's not as unusual as you may think—this can be hard stuff to articulate. If they don't know how to answer, then we'll coach them with more specific questions:

"What do you want to try to accomplish?"

"Here's where you are today, what would you like to have happen in your life?" Often people will respond with, "Personally, professionally, or financially?" My response is, "I'll go any way you want to go," because I want to understand what's on their mind and if it's personal, that's OK, too. Remember, "personal finance" is a lot more *personal* than it is finance.

We talk about hard things:

- Divorce

- Extramarital affairs

- Parents

- Kids

- Drugs

Why? Because all those things are a part of life. We don't just check questions off a list. My team has three targeted questions, and we've got to *listen* to get any value from those conversations.

What does worry do for you? Nothing.

Next we ask, "What are your fears? What keeps you up at night? What do you worry about? What causes you to lose sleep?" Some people will say, "I sleep super well." Some will say, "I'm worried about money" or "I worry about everything." Then we talk about what worrying does for that person. That question is an eye-opener: *What does worry do for you?*

I was asked recently what scripture says about worry. Scripture says worry doesn't get you one more day. It doesn't do *anything* for you. In fact, worrying is basically saying you don't trust God to be your provider.

Worry is, you could say, a sin.

That gets heavy for a client, especially if they're religious and they hear worry could potentially be sinful. But for the most part, people think about it for a minute, then agree with us.

Then we say, "All right, so you may be worried. How can I help take away your worry?" Because just telling people not to worry doesn't solve it. We hear things like:

"I'm worried about my finances because I don't like the wiggling market."

"I'm worried because I look at our finances and I just don't see how we're going to make it."

"I need to pay so many bills off, I'm worried I'll never retire."

The next step is to determine what kind of financial worry these clients might have. For example, do they have a mortgage? If the answer is yes, then let's get it paid off. A paid-off mortgage means less demand on the budget. If you have less demand on your budget, then you need *less income*. If you need less income, the remaining portfolio you have is *generating income*. If you need less income, you have more flexibility. You have more freedom.

Let's say a husband and wife come to meet with me and my team—we'll call them Betty and Mark. I'll ask Mark the first question: "Mark, when you look at Betty, what would she say is your unique talent per Coach? What would she say you do better than anyone else? What are you naturally a genius at?" Then he'll blush, "She would say I'm great managing people," or "I'm great with numbers," or something else. Then I'll pose the same question to Betty.

Sometimes we get clients who aren't ready to face the answers to these questions. If they won't share their goals, dreams, or open up about their hopes for the future with us, we can't help them. After forty years of doing this, I know what I can control. I can control what we deliver to clients. I can control how we perform, and I can control the experience clients have with us.

By contrast, I cannot control how potential clients may react, and sometimes they simply aren't ready to walk down this path.


## MEET RANDY AND DEBBIE

Meet Randy and Debbie. He's sixty-four; she's sixty-three. They haven't saved enough to retire, but they have followed our advice.

Randy is an engineer by trade but being a lifelong smoker and drinker have exacted a hefty price, and now he can't do what he was trained to do. But Randy does work. He works at Amazon, but not with Jeff Bezos. He pulls packages off the conveyor and drops them onto a pallet where robots come by and put them in the trucks.

It is unfortunate, but that's what Randy does to make ends meet. During a recent meeting, I said that he ought to consider increasing his hours from four hours a day to six or eight.

"How do you feel about that?" I asked.

"I wouldn't like it," he responded.

"Well, based on what I see today, you're going to run out of money at age eighty-five. You're going to run out of cash resources." That gave Randy pause. He and Debbie have about $400,000 and they spend about $55,000 to $60,000 a year. They get $40,000 a year from Social Security, so we're not talking about paupers. They have an $800,000 net worth, but our calculations indicate they'll burn through it from age sixty-four to eighty-five. They will run out unless Randy does something to earn more money. Debbie can't work due to a physical impairment, Crohn's disease—so it's up to Randy.

Could they have done something different earlier? Sure, but dwelling on that would be beating up on themselves. I ask, "OK, what can you do to improve yourself today for tomorrow?"

At this point, Randy and Debbie have followed our advice and now they're debt-free. Their situation isn't ideal, but they're willing and open to make the changes necessary to set themselves up for a better retirement than they thought possible.

## DEVELOPING A GAME PLAN

As I've said throughout this book, "personal finance" is a lot more *personal* than it is finance, which is why we like to meet with clients in person at least once a year. Those questions I mentioned earlier are on every agenda. That means I can pull up notes from when we first sat down and use them in our meeting. Often I'll pull up the notes from our discussion three years earlier and compare them with what a client just said, then remind them of the progress they've made.

Perhaps three years earlier a client was worried about a student loan and making the mortgage. Today the loan is paid off and the mortgage balance keeps shrinking. We've made significant progress in the past three years.

Having their finances in perspective is part of why clients feel so good when they leave our offices. We focus on progress.

It's a little like going to see a personal trainer for the first time. It doesn't matter if you're ridiculously overweight. The fact that you've gone to see a trainer gives you some confidence you're doing something about it. Maybe you've got some anxiety about having to deal with these problems. Maybe you've got a long way to go. But the fact is you're working on it.

When you're working with someone who wants to be by your side and help you accomplish your goals, no matter the current scenario, you're going to feel better. Because at least you've decided to do something and be accountable to someone—to partner with someone to help make that happen.

We call our financial plan a *game plan* because it's light, flexible, and creates accountability. It asks tough questions, but it's not fixed in a 300-page binder that goes to binder heaven—a.k.a., the back of a client's closet or the shredder.

A game plan is three to five pages. It's a review of what you want to achieve along with recommendations for your portfolio. It also outlines what we're going to implement—think of it like a checklist of things to do. Then there's a full disclosure, including costs and our fee structure. Then, we outline what implementation will look like: the type of companies that we're going to own for the client, our investment philosophy, the strategy, and finally, what to expect going forward.

We don't charge for a game plan, either. Some people say that's silly. Frankly, that's the way we've done it. It works. I'm not in business to maximize the return on advisor. Our goal is to solve problems and to help people become more independent and have more freedom—of time, resources, and choices. That's why we do what we do.

I believe plenty of people out there need and want what we do. But we're not trying to be McDonald's and appeal to any and every person. We're trying to carefully *solve client problems*. By listening to clients and their concerns, we develop solutions and strategies. That gives clients the freedom to go live and do the kinds of things they want to do.

Clients need to be ready to work with us. If you don't want my advice and I keep giving it to you, it's just going to be frustrating for you. If you don't want to follow our advice, it's going to be frustrating for me because you've chosen not to do what we've advised.

If clients want to know what their financial future will look like in ten years, I can't really help them. It's a little paradoxical: the best way to prepare for ten to twenty years of retirement is to work toward three-year milestones. Saving for retirement is hard for a lot of people because they are putting money away for an event far down the line.

When a twenty-six-year-old saves $5,000 in her 401(k) and we show her how that money will grow, it's easy to understand the benefit. But we also show her that five grand might feel like a lot, but really, even if it doubles, she is still not going to have much. The hard part is getting the twenty-six-year-old to cough up the extra funds and put them away for retirement.

Saving for retirement is deferred gratification, and our culture doesn't embrace that. We point out to people that if they don't save a sufficient amount, then retirement at age sixty-five might not be an option. The choices made today will make, or break, your ability to retire with dignity and more options.

Potential clients *must want something better* and be willing to work with us toward that goal. If you have a bad experience in your financial life, the key is to learn from it and change your activity. My team can help you with that. If you keep repeating the same behavior, then you've wasted the opportunity to learn from your mistakes.

It takes a lifetime to learn how to live.

CHAPTER EIGHT

# Final Thoughts

I hope at this point you're ready to take the next steps toward a brighter financial future. If you've read this book and understand our message, that's great! However, if you set the book aside, never to be referenced again, that's disappointing. If our message hasn't convinced you to take action, you're postponing your duties to yourself and your family.

Don't procrastinate. You own your future; you can create your future. Make it a priority—now! Because the sooner you do, the better off you'll be.

It's so easy to put things like personal finance off—life gets in the way—but your future should be a priority. Obviously no one is forcing you to take care of your financial future. It's up to you to make that decision.

But if I may make the case for acting now, I think you'll be happier for it. Thinking about taking definitive action "someday" is too late. It's the worst thing you could do. "Better late than never" simply *does not apply* to planning for retirement. Growing your income is essential, especially if you're planning to enjoy retirement and make work a choice.

In other words, if you want a life filled with options, your assets *need to be generating income.*

I am so gratified to help my clients move toward a sustainable and rewarding retirement. Recently, I was asked if there's a demographic we prefer to serve.

"No," I answered. "Every client is different, and every plan for every client is different." Everyone has different needs, and we're sensitive to that.

Buddy and Judy are a good example. They've been clients since 1978. Originally I helped them file and solve a claim on a limited partnership. He's a pediatrician and she was an attorney-turned-full-time mom. They didn't have a lot, but they worked hard and followed our advice. They colored inside the lines we drew for them way back then.

"I don't know how to take care of this money, my retirement money. I'm a doctor. I want to take care of kids," Buddy said to me, and I made sure to set up a plan that suited his future needs. Now they're incredibly blessed. They've had the freedom to do everything they've dreamed about doing.

Buddy and Judy are in their eighties now and have a loving family. They were good savers, even when it was hard to put money aside. They followed our advice. The financial markets blessed them, and now this couple can pass those blessings along to their family and the charities of their choice—and that's what they've chosen to do. Their two children grew up and had children, and because this couple made smart financial choices throughout their lives, their children and grandchildren benefit.

Why did that happen? I don't know why God put me in their lives, or them in mine. I just know we helped them. As crazy as it sounds, I get huge emotional and spiritual satisfaction out of helping people. That's why I do what I do.

Our ideal client is one who makes the smart choice: following through on the advice we give. Do all our clients follow our advice? Probably 99 percent of them do. For those who don't, all we can do is shrug our shoulders and say, "It looks like you're digging a hole. We would suggest you stop digging." Some do, some don't.

Everything is about choices. You can choose to follow our advice or not. Our ideal client made choices. They sought advice. They followed it. They developed a financial game plan. They implemented it, and in the process said no to some things. Investing for your future is really all about delayed gratification—saying no to spending in the present.

Now is a great time to start making some of these smart decisions. Get an idea of what's important to you, then start making choices to reflect those priorities. We're here to help you lay out, make sense of, and inform those choices. The right choices today mean more freedom in the future. Freedom from having to work in retirement gives you the flexibility to do the things you want to do.

If you choose to work with an advisor or a professional, try to find someone who really cares about you, your situation, and what makes sense for you. Our mantra here is "Care beyond advice."

A lot of bad actors are out there giving financial advice. But many other people are really trying to do right by their clients. The latter type of advisor certainly won't use gimmicks to entice clients. It's really a measure of their character. Unfortunately, you can't really demonstrate or measure character on a website. You can't measure it on a government evaluation. You must measure character by interviewing and getting to know people. It's only after you've gotten to know those people, worked with them, and weathered both good and stormy experiences that you really begin to understand their character.

Good advisors do what it takes to get through challenges. They also give you advice—but not always what you might want to hear. Likewise, in good times, great advisors don't beat their chests. They typically say, "Well, that's what the markets do—they reward investors. They reward people who are patient." Being able to provide for your family is like putting an exclamation point on life. Why not start today?

# EPILOGUE

Investing and ownership is a passion for me. I have had the blessing that this is my "first job." I was hired right out of college by EF Hutton. I have researched, tried, and followed nearly every investment alternative. Through lots of trial and error, and plenty of lessons learned, I have found that dividend investing works.

The great thing about our country is investors have the freedom to chase trends, new ideas, strategies—all in an attempt to ultimately beat the market, or build up what I call a "retirement pile." Frankly, trying to buy low, sell high, and reinvest in something that is low priced, and then to have that happen again and again, sounds like a lot of work—and it is. I have also never seen anyone who has the ability to do this with any degree of consistency.

Capital appreciation or growth is an unreliable source of income. I think growth of income investing with dividend-paying companies is a secret few on Wall Street embrace. It's boring. But bore me to death with income that can double every seven to ten years, where I don't need to worry about the daily, weekly, monthly, or even yearly value of my investment! What I do pay attention to are those dividend increases and larger checks.

Dividends may not be the only way to invest for investor success, but if there is a better one, I have yet to find it.

CPSIA information can be obtained
at www.ICGtesting.com
Printed in the USA
BVHW042110120319
542318BV00040B/1193/P

9 781949 639629